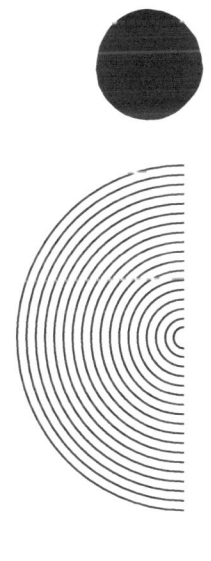

WHIRLYGIG

INSIDE BOB DYLAN'S
TIME OUT OF MIND SESSIONS

john lewis

Illustrations by Warren Linn

Creative Direction and Design by
Amanda White-Iseli

COPYRIGHT © 2022 JOHN LEWIS

All rights reserved. No part of this book may be reproduced in any form without permission of the publisher, except by reviewers, who may quote brief passages.

ISBN 978-0-578-36117-8

Library of Congress Control Number 2022901315

John Lewis, author
Whirly Gig: Inside Bob Dylan's Time Out of Mind *Sessions* / Analysis of the creative process and Jim Dickinson's role in the making of Bob Dylan's 1997 album / John Lewis.
—First edition.

Printed in the United States of America
First printing May 2022

Published by Dorchester Power and Light
www.dorchpowerandlight.com

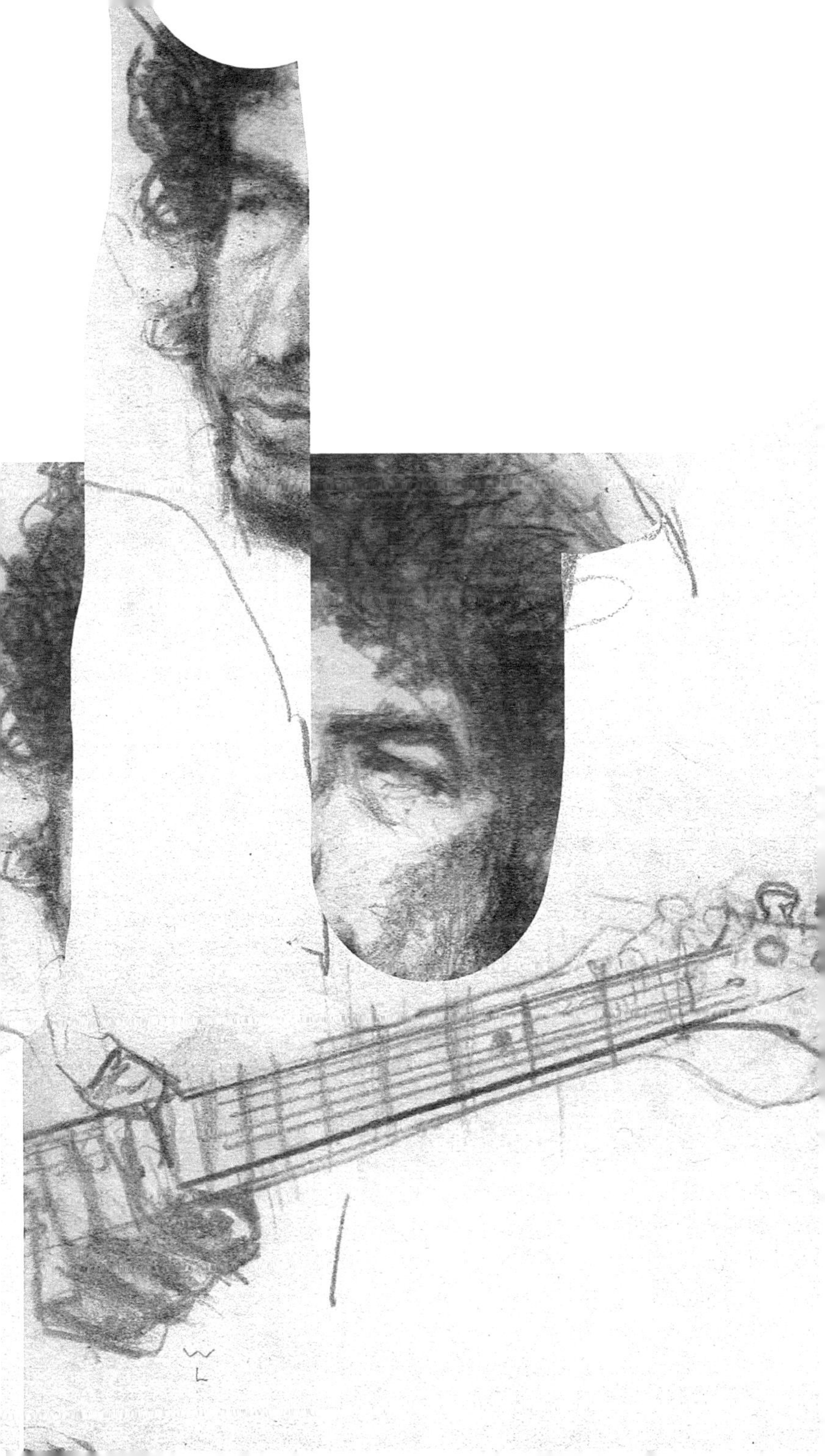
W
L

VOLUME VIBRATO

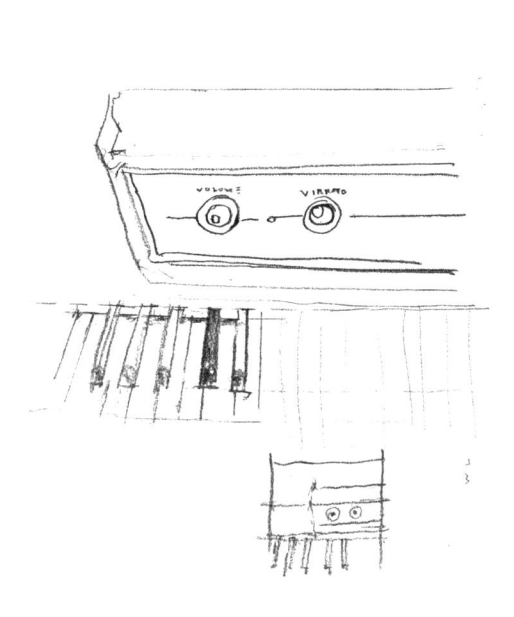

DEDICATED TO THE SPIRIT OF JIM DICKINSON

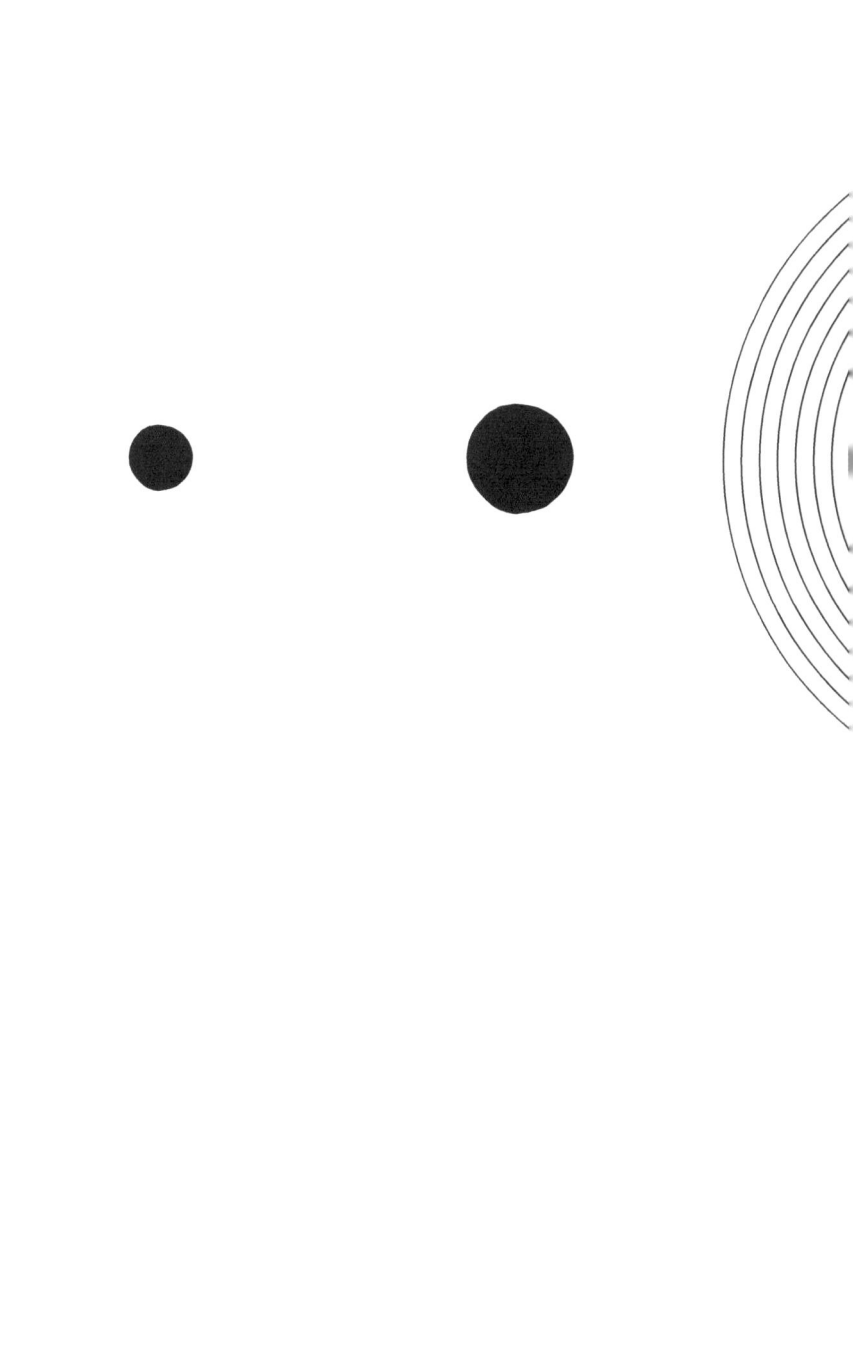

JERRY WEXLER WAS FOND OF SAYING,

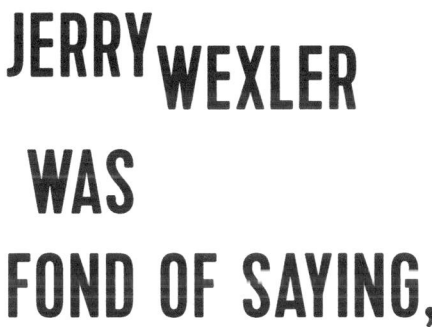

"You never know who is going to produce a record. It might be the guy who comes in with the coffee." Wexler, a legendary figure at Atlantic Records, knew his way around a recording studio, having helmed seminal sessions by Ray Charles, Aretha Franklin, and Bob Dylan (*Slow Train Coming*). He certainly wasn't going to cede production credit to the coffee guy, but Wexler understood how the presence of a single person, someone beyond the producer's control, could profoundly alter the mood, feel, or soul of a session.

Wexler wasn't involved in recording Dylan's *Time Out of Mind*, but the tapes from those sessions prove his point. *Time Out of Mind* famously resurrected Dylan's career, commercially and critically, and producer Daniel Lanois got a good bit of the credit. Lanois was, after all, well known for his distinctive, meticulously layered production on blockbuster records such as U2's *The Joshua Tree* and Peter Gabriel's *So*, as well as low-key favorites like Emmylou Harris's *Wrecking Ball* and The Neville Brothers' *Yellow Moon*. Lanois also cut his teeth working on ambient records by Brian Eno, adding, most notably, the otherworldly pedal steel guitar to *Apollo: Atmospheres and Soundtracks*.

I spent a week listening to session tapes at the Bob Dylan Archive in Tulsa, and it's apparent that Jim Dickinson also deserves credit for profoundly shaping *Time Out of Mind*. Dickinson became a key Dylan ally and confidant during the recording process and infused the record, tangibly and intangibly, with soulful ballast. He brought the coffee.

HE BROUGHT THE COFFEE.

In fact, by the time Dickinson turned up to play keyboards at the sessions in Miami, Dylan and Lanois weren't even speaking to one another. They were fighting over the album's direction and engaged in something of a tit-for-tat accumulation of session players. There were even a few violent outbursts. *Time Out of Mind* is a great album in spite of Lanois, not because of him.

I came to that conclusion in Tulsa, though I'm not totally unbiased. I knew Jim Dickinson and considered him a friend. I profiled Jim for *The Oxford American*, wrote about his Screamin' Jay Hawkins sessions in Memphis for *Rolling Stone*, and talked to him every few weeks for a decade before he passed away in 2009. Equal parts oral historian and gifted storyteller, Jim was refreshingly candid and committed to sharing his experiences working with The Rolling Stones, Aretha Franklin, Big Star, and many others.

Keith Richards admired Jim as a musician and raconteur. In his autobiography, *Life*, the legendary guitarist relied largely on Jim's account of the Muscle Shoals recording sessions that generated classics such as "Brown Sugar" and "Wild Horses." Jim famously played piano on the latter tune and recounted the experience with mythic swagger. Keith recognized a kindred spirit.

So did Dylan. In his memoir, *Chronicles*, he wrote that Jim came to mind while recording *Oh Mercy*:

> If I had to do this again, I would have brought somebody with me, somebody that went back a ways—someone who I liked as a musician, who had ideas and could play them, who had come down the same musical path as me. Lately I'd been thinking about Jim Dickinson and how it would have been good to have him here. . . . We had a lot of things in common and it would have been good to have him around.

So Dylan had Dickinson in mind while working on an earlier album that, not coincidentally, was also produced by Daniel Lanois. The next time Dylan went into the studio with Lanois, Dickinson would be there.

During the decade or so preceding *Time Out of Mind*, Dylan struggled mightily. He seemed baffled by new technologies, the rise of MTV, and the emergence of rap. The synthesizer was not his friend, nor was the music video, as Paul Shrader's "Tight Connection To My Heart" made clear. Collaborations with Kurtis Blow and hip-hop collective Full Force were ill-conceived, and Dylan slid steadily down the charts and saw his creative aura dim. 1988's *Down in the Groove*, for instance, peaked at #70 on the albums chart, with critic Robert Christgau deriding it as "horrendous product." Tours with Tom Petty and The Grateful Dead were largely uninspired affairs, hinting at past glories but showing no way forward.

Dylan eventually intuited that stripping things down and getting back to his roots would set him on the right path. In 1988, he pared down his touring band to a lean trio and embarked on what's become known as *The Never Ending Tour*. With guitarist G.E. Smith as bandleader, Dylan dug into his catalogue, rearranged classic songs, and worked up obscure traditional tunes. On any given night, he'd play "The Lonesome Death of Hattie Carroll" or a revamped "Tangled Up In Blue" alongside "The Wagoner's Lad" and "Trail of the Buffalo." He practically ignored his 1980s material.

When Dylan got the notion to record again, he didn't lay down a batch of new songs with the latest gear and an all-star band. Instead, he recorded old folk tunes on acoustic guitar and harmonica, like it was 1962 rather than 1992, in his garage. The resulting album, *Good As I Been to You*, and a companion LP, 1993's *World Gone Wrong*, were logical extensions of the covers enlivening Dylan's concerts, an important shift from the trendy to the timeless. Finally, he was playing the long game.

It was years before Dylan returned to the studio to record *Time Out of Mind*. When he did, he claimed to have written new material for his younger fans, but these tunes seemed directed at his peers staring down the past and confronting mortality. The songs were infused with a rough-hewn dignity that comes with survival.

I journeyed to Tulsa hoping to gain an understanding of how the songs developed and evolved over time. Jim told me the transfor-

> THE AUDIO RANGED FROM SKELETAL DEMOS TO POLISHED MIXES AND EVEN INCLUDED DYLAN AND LANOIS'S BETWEEN-SONGS BANTER. IT WAS REVELATORY.

mation was profound, but the process was shrouded in mystery, and I had little sense of how it actually happened. That began to change the minute I settled into my seat at the archive and librarian Mark Davidson brought out the items I'd requested: folders full of Dylan's handwritten lyrics, notes scribbled on scraps of paper, related correspondence, and recording studio documentation, as well as 500-plus audio files culled from the sessions. The audio ranged from skeletal demos to polished mixes and even included Dylan and Lanois's between-songs banter. It was revelatory.

Over the course of a week sifting through the material, I came to understand how *Time Out of Mind* became such a gem. I even identified the moment when the chaotic sessions coalesced into a thing of real beauty. It happened when Dickinson entered the room.

After opting to record again with Lanois, Dylan suggested the producer listen to blues greats Charley Patton and Little Walter prior to the sessions. Dylan was reportedly fascinated by Beck, who'd just released *Odelay*, and Lanois ran with that notion. During pre-production at The Teatro, Lanois's studio in Oxnard, California, Lanois and Tony Mangurian played percussion over Patton songs, then deleted the Patton parts and created loops from their drumming. Lanois intended to use the loops with Dylan's new material to construct layered, beat-heavy tunes.

I EVEN IDENTIFIED
THE MOMENT
WHEN THE CHAOTIC SESSIONS
COALESCED
INTO
A THING
OF REAL BEAUTY.
IT HAPPENED WHEN

DICKINSON ENTERED THE ROOM.

But Lanois had, unwittingly, removed the most important element: the Patton. He was likely dazzled by the electronics, the heady cut-and-paste of Beck's approach rather than the blues at its heart. As it turned out, Dylan had other ideas.

Listening to the Oxnard tapes in Tulsa, it's apparent Dylan was wary of Lanois's approach, which relied heavily on digital processing and extensive overdubbing. When Dylan arrived at The Teatro in the fall of 1996, he found himself alone with Lanois and Mangurian. "What do you do around here for musicians?" he asked Lanois.

Dylan sensed, early on, that a lack of human touch would circumvent the songs' power. He wasn't comfortable simply turning them over to Lanois. "Do you just play everything yourself?" Dylan asked point blank. Lanois responded non-committally, saying they hadn't completed many projects at the studio.

I can imagine Dylan narrowing his eyes and nodding, not in agreement, but like something was dawning on him. For much of the previous decade, he'd been circling back to American myths, searching for lost chords, and barnstorming around the country like the troubadours he admired. Did he really, at the age of 55, want to make a Beck record?

For a few weeks, Dylan and Lanois bounced ideas off one another and did a lot of noodling. Primitive renderings of the songs emerged, but the beats and loops approach never took hold with Dylan. It's a good thing, because some of that material sounded like scuzzy Jon Spencer outtakes, and the lack of clear direction, or shared vision, proved divisive.

While working on an early version of "Not Dark Yet," Lanois urged Dylan to "nail this big piano riff." Dylan, who'd been giving it a gospel feel, not only demurred, he suggested Lanois play the riff himself "like how Carl Perkins would play it." It was no offhand comment. Dylan knew that Perkins, the rockabilly pioneer who recorded

IT'S A GOOD THING, BECAUSE SOME OF THAT MATERIAL SOUNDED LIKE SCUZZY JON SPENCER OUTTAKES, AND THE LACK OF CLEAR DIRECTION, OR SHARED VISION, PROVED DIVISIVE.

for Sun Records in the 1950s, wasn't a natural reference point for Lanois. He didn't suggest Lanois play it like U2's The Edge or some other heavily processed guitarist. The comment hinted at an old school approach that figured to unsettle Lanois, who must have sensed Dylan was getting restless.

One afternoon, they were working out a part and Dylan set aside his guitar and announced, "I think I'm gonna split early."

"You're gonna split?" asked Lanois, clearly baffled.

"Yeah," Dylan told him, "I'm gonna meet... looks like I gotta be someplace before dark."

Dylan sounded like he'd had enough for the day, or maybe he'd had enough of the Oxnard experiment. I suspect he wasn't just offering an excuse for knocking off early; he sensed there really was a date he needed to keep, someone he needed to meet, before it was too late. The lyrics waltzing around his head conveyed something to that effect: "It's not dark yet, but..."

Lanois may have been hearing Beck's "Devil's Haircut" in his mind, but Dylan heard something else entirely. He heard a voice beckoning him to some mythical destination like Memphis or the Mississippi crossroads where musicians of his ilk didn't cut trendy records— they cut deals with Satan to attain heavenly results.

A struggle for the soul of *Time Out of Mind* had begun.

A STRUGGLE FOR THE SOUL OF TIME OUT OF MIND HAD BEGUN.

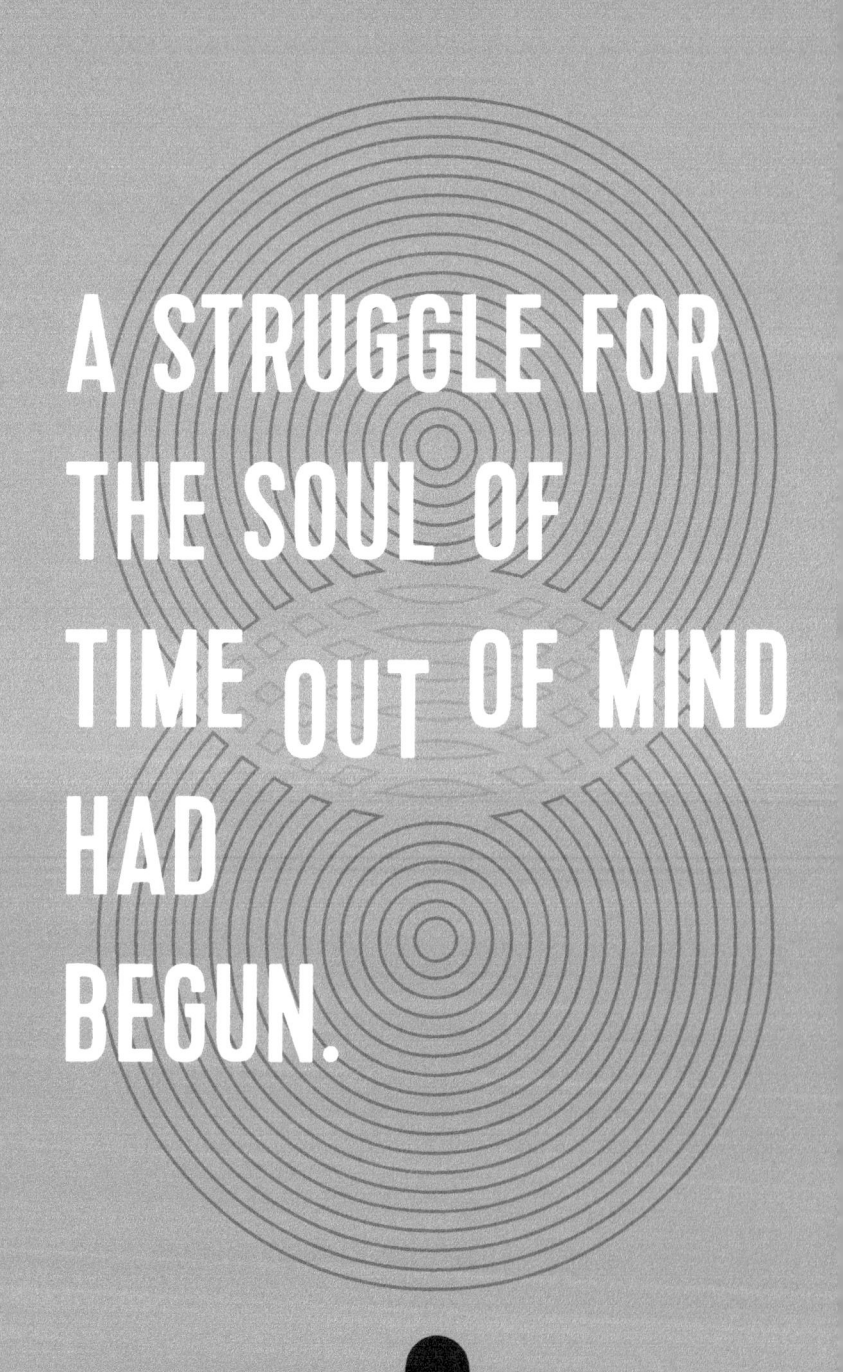

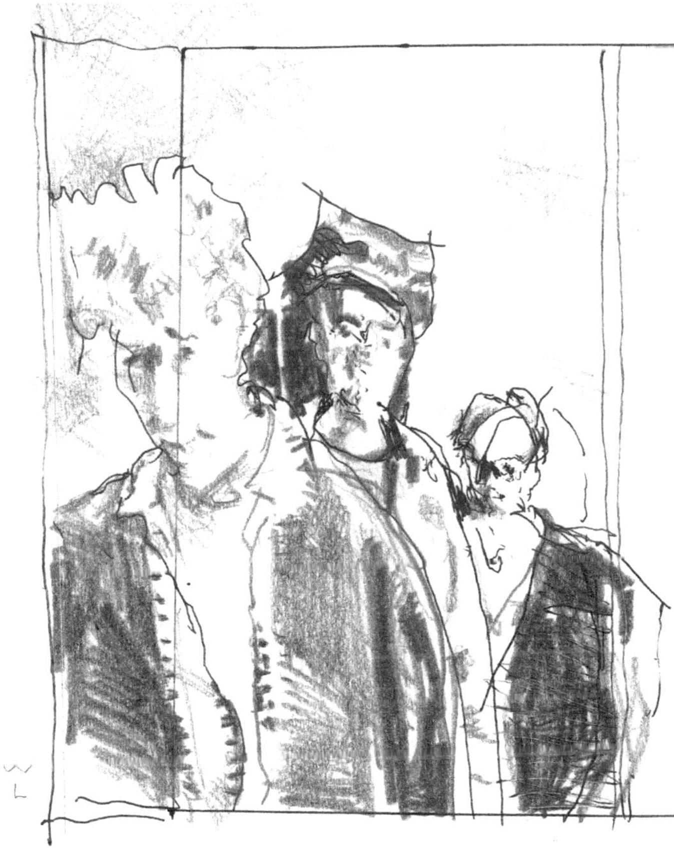

Dylan decided to change studios, which Lanois found unsettling. Lanois felt The Teatro had the best vibe, which makes sense considering it was his studio. He also knew that recording there gave him the best shot at controlling the project and layering and tinkering to his heart's content.

Dylan relocated as far as he could get from Lanois's studio, heading 3,000 miles from Oxnard to Criteria Recording Studios in Miami. To Lanois and his engineer, Mark Howard, the studio conjured gold and platinum blockbusters such as *Hotel California*, *Rumours*, and the *Saturday Night Fever* soundtrack, all recorded at Criteria. It likely had other associations for Dylan. It was where The Allman Brothers finished *Eat a Peach* after Duane died, Eric Clapton recorded "Layla," and James Brown recorded "I Got You (I Feel Good)." It's where Aretha Franklin cut *Spirit in the Dark*, when Criteria's house band, The Dixie Flyers, featured Dickinson on keyboards.

At Criteria, Dickinson recorded his solo debut, *Dixie Fried*, which took its name from a Carl Perkins song. Writer Nick Tosches called that record "one of the most bizarrely powerful musics of this century," and Wexler once claimed that if Dylan had made *Dixie Fried*, "They'd call him the risen Christ."

Dylan wanted *that* Criteria.

He also wanted to record with his road band, the guys he played with every night: bassist Tony Garnier, pedal steel guitarist Bucky Baxter, and drummer David Kemper. He wanted to ditch the cut-and-paste collage approach.

And what was Lanois thinking? The tapes from the early sessions at Criteria suggest he wanted to make *Blonde on Blonde* 2.0.

When the group assembled on January 2, 1997, Dylan hadn't yet arrived, so Lanois ran down the new material with the band. It was a fresh start, and he could have taken it in any number of directions. Listening to that day's session tapes, it's baffling to hear him hearken back to what Dylan was doing 30 years earlier. Lanois had tried something similar while making *Oh Mercy*, by repeatedly suggesting

DYLAN WANTED
THAT CRITERIA.

WHEN DYLAN WALKED INTO CRITERIA TO BEGIN RECORDING THE FOLLOWING DAY, THE STAGE WAS SET FOR CONFUSION AND CONFLICT. LANOIS WAS CHARTING A COURSE BACKWARDS. IT WASN'T THE DIRECTION DYLAN WAS HEADED.

Dylan write "new" songs that sounded like "Masters of War," "Girl from the North Country," or "God on Our Side." Dylan, in *Chronicles*, stated flatly that he "didn't have anything like those songs."

Lanois led the band through "Not Dark Yet," "Dirt Road Blues," and "Red River Shore," ascending through upper registers and building to crescendos that peaked during Dylan's 1966 tour with The Band. Twisting them into buoyant anthems was downright bizarre, considering the lyrics Dylan was crafting. Even stranger, Lanois imitated Dylan's singing and added his own lyrics along the way.

> Oh mama, listen to what I have have to sayyyy
> The boys have all come down to learn how to pray
> They got sand in their shoes and dust in their eyyyyes
> They don't wanna hearrrrr no more lies.

And the chorus: "He said to me, 'It's not dark yet, Danny boy, but it's gettin' there.'"

The band may have found it cheeky—sending up the boss behind his back—but it's disorienting to hear Dylan's first new material of the 1990s treated as a nostalgia trip. But as the song ended, Lanois seemed pleased: "Well, that sounds pretty cool," he told the band.

When Dylan walked into Criteria to begin recording the following day, the stage was set for confusion and conflict. Lanois was charting a course backwards. It wasn't the direction Dylan was headed.

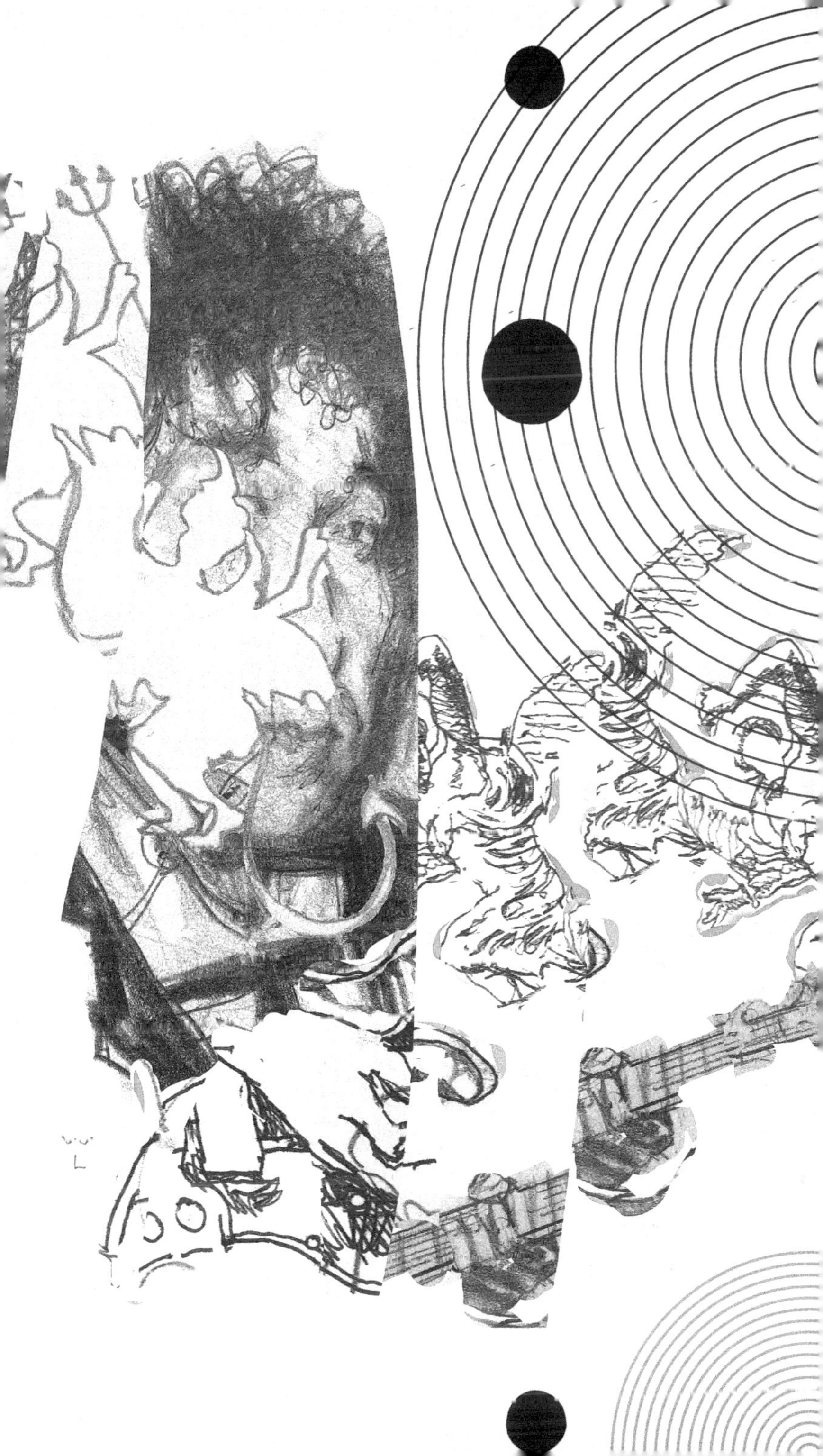

The early sessions at Criteria did not go well. As Dylan explored bluesy, lower keys more suitable for his lyrics and frame of mind, Lanois attempted to salvage a few beats from the Oxnard sessions and lure Dylan back to those voice-of-his-generation anthems. Once again, "Not Dark Yet" proved problematic. On the January 5th rough mix, Dylan complained the song was "way too fast," and Lanois recommended bringing it "down two notches," which did not appease Dylan.

"What are we gonna do, put that beat to it now?" Dylan fired back.

"Yeah," said Lanois.

After a few more takes, Dylan halted the proceedings to ask, perhaps rhetorically, "Are we any closer to it?"

"Let's try it with the crescendos," suggested Lanois, but that didn't work either.

When "Can't Wait" also bogged down, Lanois resorted to his stock in trade: cool, detached ambience. This version of "Can't Wait" was dubbed the "psychedelic" version in the session documents. After the first minute and a half, it sounds downright Floyd-ian with comfortably numb guitar licks and, a few minutes later, pedal steel that feels beamed in from Eno's 1983 *Apollo*. The instrumentation drifts moodily, with no grit or gravitas, unmoored from lyrics that could, at this point, be interpreted as commentary on Lanois's flailing. . . .

> It's got to end
> Everything about it just feels wrong
> I'll be dead
> Bein' close to her is where I don't belong
> Well my back is to the sun
> Cause the light is too intense
> I can see what everybody in the world is up against
> That's how it is, when things disintegrate
> And I don't know how much longer I can wait

As the sessions continued, Lanois grew volatile. He reportedly smashed a guitar while working on *Oh Mercy*, and similarly

AS THE SESSIONS CONTINUED, LANOIS GREW VOLATILE. HE REPORTEDLY SMASHED A GUITAR WHILE WORKING ON *OH MERCY*, AND SIMILARLY VIOLENT OUTBURSTS FOLLOWED AT CRITERIA.

violent outbursts followed at Criteria. Lanois, at various points, hurled a metal stool that knocked out the control room lights, kicked and dented the recording console, and slammed a studio door so hard the glass shattered, leading Dylan to ask if he had some sort of problem. Dylan, at one point, threatened retaliation by picking up Lanois's dobro and swinging it overhead, a not-so-veiled reference to the *Oh Mercy* incident that suggested he could do some guitar smashing of his own.

As all this played out, both men summoned additional musicians: Lanois called in drummer Brian Blade, Dylan brought aboard session legend Jim Keltner. The ranks swelled to nearly a dozen players, including keyboardist Augie Meyers, and guitarists Bob Britt, Cindy Cashdollar, and Duke Robillard, in addition to the road band (Baxter, Garnier, and Kemper), Lanois, and Dylan.

It might have been complete chaos, but Dylan and Lanois managed to keep things from getting out of hand and the material began taking shape. Meyers proved to be a steadying influence, adding his trademark organ to spry versions of "Dirt Road Blues" and "Tryin' to Get to Heaven." Lanois told Meyers and guitarist Bucky Baxter they "should be thinking like one. Ultimately, you guys will have a similar sound. You're like one instrument."

AS "MISSISSIPPI" SLOWED ON SUBSEQUENT TAKES, THE LYRICS SHARPENED SOMEWHAT, BUT IT STILL DIDN'T FEEL RIGHT. . . . TWO DAYS LATER, HE SUMMONED JIM DICKINSON.

As a result, certain parts coalesced, and the ensemble played more cohesively. Lanois lauded the "orchestra drumming" on a "Love Sick" take that featured Cashdollar adding a moody theremin sound. "Not Dark Yet" eventually downshifted to a steady tempo, though it still suffered from noodling—Lanois asked to have his guitar "up front in the mix" on the January 11 version—and booming drums. Dylan can be heard complaining about being "confused on the beat."

"Cold Irons Bound" settled into an atmospheric rumble with a goth-ish electric guitar on one unfortunate take. "Well, the song is there," Dylan noted. "Don't know if we're hittin' it right."

"Mississippi," much like "Can't Wait," continued to lack focus. Its jaunty Tex-Mex feel trampled over poignant lines such as "you can always come back, but you can't come back all the way." Dylan may have been tempted to call in Al Kooper; his old pal's name and phone number were scribbled on a "Mississippi" lyric sheet that's archived in Tulsa.

As "Mississippi" slowed on subsequent takes, the lyrics sharpened somewhat, but it still didn't feel right. "There's something a little too sunny about it," Dylan observed on January 11.

Two days later, he summoned Jim Dickinson.

STAYED IN MISSISSIPPI A DAY TOO LONG

(FROM DYLAN'S "MISSISSIPPI")

DOWN IN MISSISSIPPI WHERE I BELONG

(FROM DICKINSON'S SIGNATURE SONG, "DOWN IN MISSISSIPPI")

WHIRLY GIG

Dickinson wasn't simply a hired hand. He was a larger-than-life, though largely unknown, presence in American music. Jim joked that if he could have capoed the piano, he'd have had a better career. He was more magician than musician, a shamanic conjurer of crippled chords that resonated at gutbucket frequencies. He possessed an intangible, elusive quality that was legendary amongst in-the-know musicians.

Novelist Walter Mosley could have been writing about Jim when, in *RL's Dream*, he described his blues-playing protagonist as having "music in his shoulders and down in his feet. . . . Not that pretty even stuff that they box in radios and stereos. Not even something that you can catch in a beat. It's the earth moving and babies looking from side to side."

I visited Jim at his Mississippi home and got a sense of exactly that. After introducing me to his wife, Mary Lindsay, in the double-wide trailer they shared with a beloved basset hound, he ushered me to his "fortress of solitude." Along the way, he pointed out the

> **HE WAS MORE MAGICIAN THAN MUSICIAN, A SHAMANIC CONJURER OF CRIPPLED CHORDS THAT RESONATED AT GUTBUCKET FREQUENCIES.**

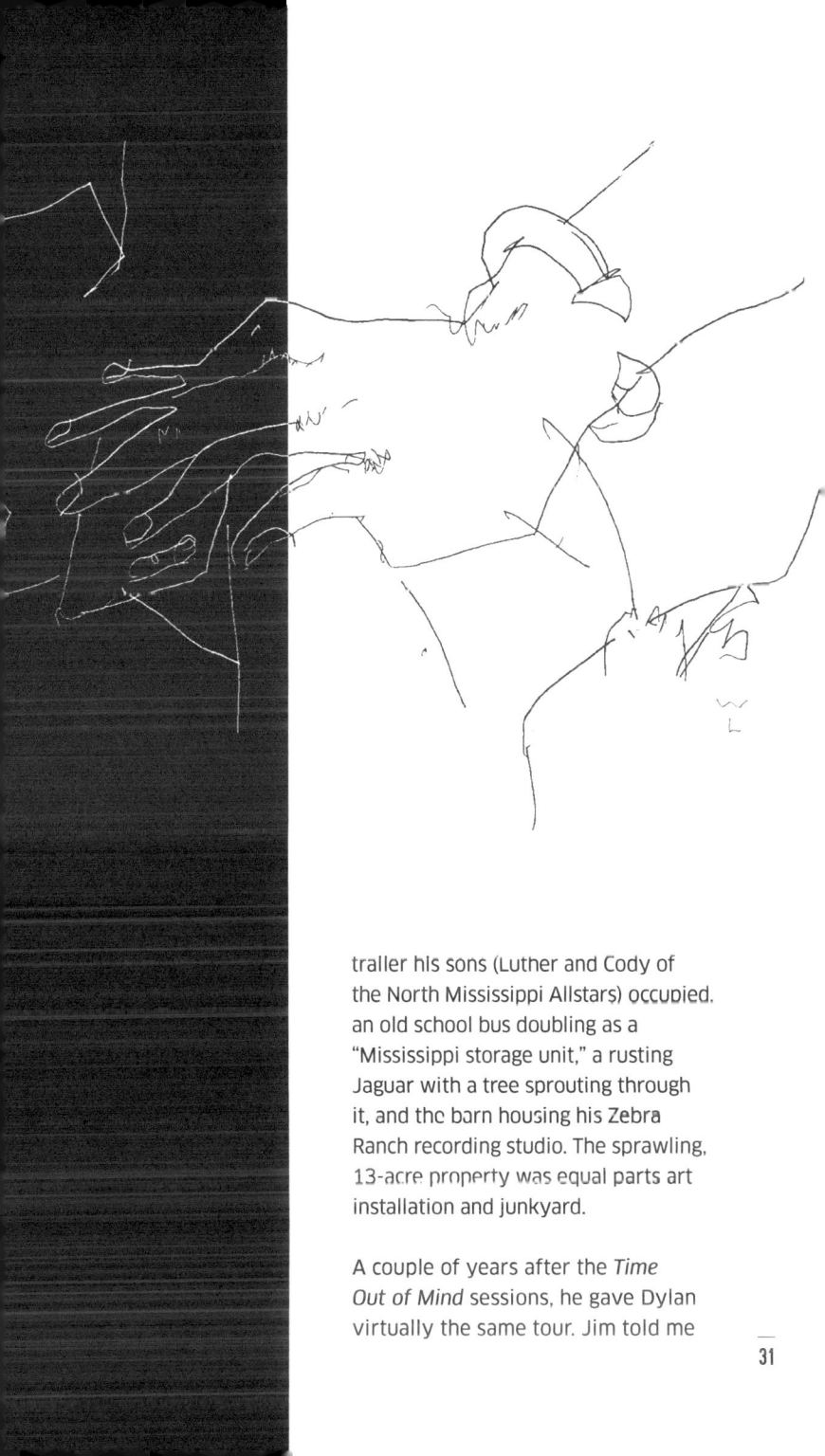

trailer his sons (Luther and Cody of
the North Mississippi Allstars) occupied,
an old school bus doubling as a
"Mississippi storage unit," a rusting
Jaguar with a tree sprouting through
it, and the barn housing his Zebra
Ranch recording studio. The sprawling,
13-acre property was equal parts art
installation and junkyard.

A couple of years after the *Time Out of Mind* sessions, he gave Dylan virtually the same tour. Jim told me

"I'LL BET YOU CAN DO A LOT OF THINKING

about firing up his El Camino and fetching Dylan from Memphis' French Quarter Hotel. Dylan said he'd like to either ride around Memphis or down into Mississippi, so Jim opted for the latter. As they turned off rural Route 51 near Jim's house, Dylan said he'd grown up in the country and his uncles were fishermen. "I hate fish," he said. He asked Jim if he knew Mississippi writer Larry Brown and claimed to have read all of Brown's books.

Walking around Zebra Ranch, Dylan, who apparently lives in a similar type of compound (minus the double-wide, I'm guessing) in California, seemed impressed. "It looks like you have everything a man could possibly want," he quipped to Dickinson. "I'll bet you can do a lot of thinking out here."

As the "fortress of solitude" name indicates, Jim was a DC Comics guy—who stacked Batman comic books next to the Zebra Ranch commode—and a thinker. He could riff about the Dark Knight's inner turmoil, and then, as a former theater major at Baylor, discuss Bertolt Brecht or southern-lit titans like Flannery O'Connor and William Faulkner. He even recorded a spoken-word album, *Fishing with Charlie*, featuring favorite pieces by Langston Hughes and Tennessee Williams.

Inside the cabin-like fortress during my first visit, Dickinson settled into a leather chair, pulled a Moroccan hash knife from his boot, and cut a few slices of a potent rum cake. A boombox sat on a nearby table alongside stacks of CDs that included some of Jim's personal favorites like *Moondog* and Miles's *Sketches of Spain*. There were many discs he produced or played on over the years: the Sun Records box set (he sings on "Cadillac Man," a late rockabilly gem), Big Star's

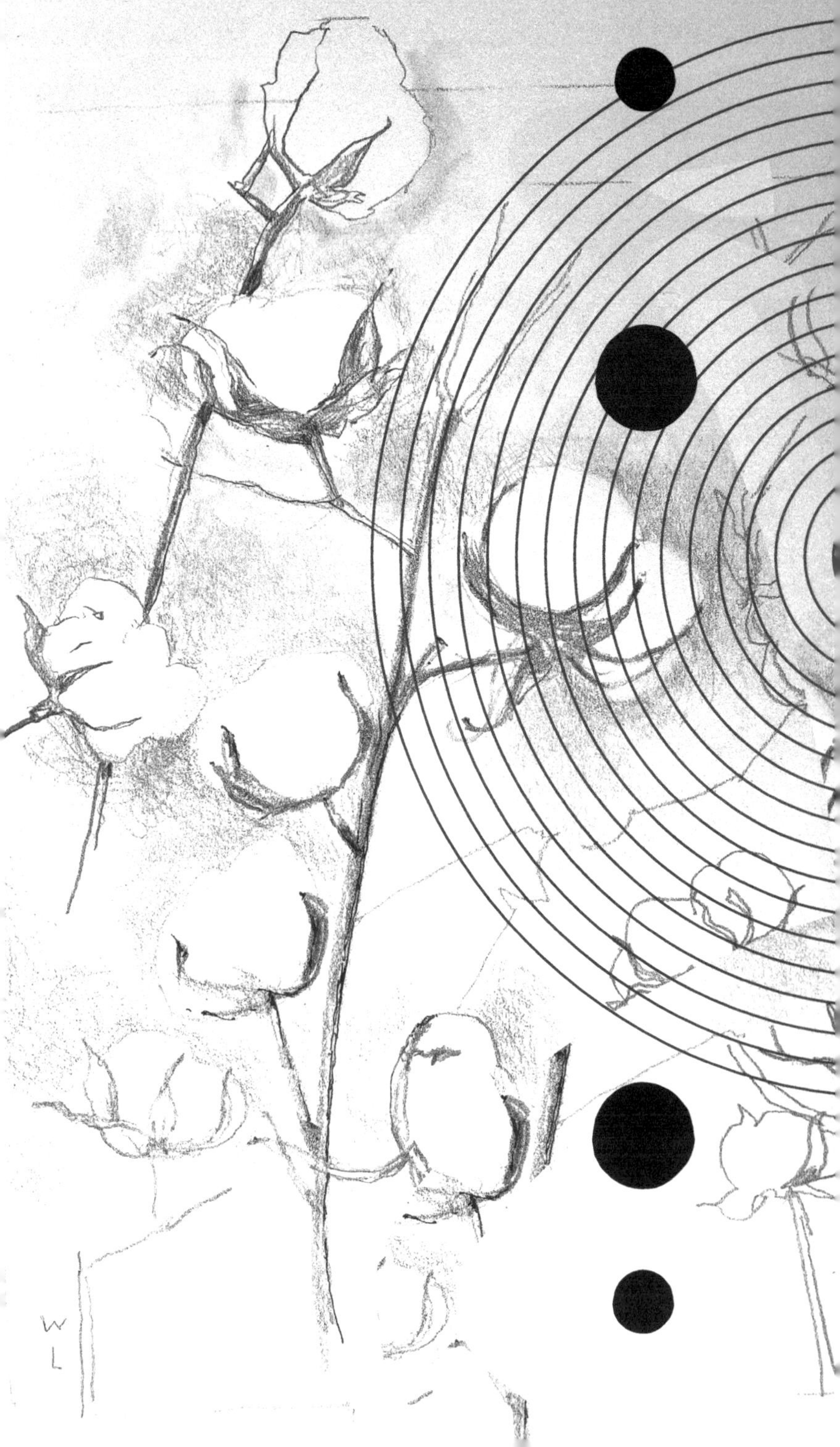
W
L

> (JIM) CONSIDERED HILL COUNTRY LEGEND OTHAR TURNER A FRIEND AND INSPIRATION. . . . "HIS MUSIC CONTAINS A COMPLETE BELIEF SYSTEM OF PHILOSOPHY AND RELIGION."

Third, Albert Collins's *Trash Talkin'*, various Ry Cooder albums and soundtracks, Arlo Guthrie's *Hobo's Lullaby*, Toots Hibbert's *Toots in Memphis*, The Replacements' *Pleased to Meet Me*, The Stones' *Sticky Fingers*, and the *Dead Man Walking* soundtrack (he plays on the Johnny Cash cut) among them.

Jim performed with blues greats Furry Lewis and Sleepy John Estes, as well as early rock icons Chuck Berry and Little Richard. He considered hill country legend Othar Turner a friend and inspiration. Turner played the cane fife and worked the fields of a farm in nearby Senatobia, where life revolved around family, friends, and his homestead. As a result, "his music contains a complete belief system of philosophy and religion," said Dickinson. "A more successful and complete human being I have never known."

On the surface, it's an impressive resume, but digging deeper into the list of credits, it's apparent that many of the albums Jim played on were transitional projects. He had an uncanny knack for turning up at key points in rock history as a transformational presence.

During his Screamin' Jay Hawkins sessions at Sam Phillips's studio in 1997, I watched Jim get on the keyboard, lay down a groove, and instruct drummer Roger Hawkins and bassist David Hood to play along. Then, he returned to the control room and removed the keyboard part. It transformed the track, as Hawkins and Hood locked into a ghosted groove that wasn't audible, but you could *feel* it.

"HE HAD AN UNCANNY KNACK FOR TURNING UP AT KEY POINTS IN ROCK HISTORY AS A TRANSFORMATIONAL PRESENCE."

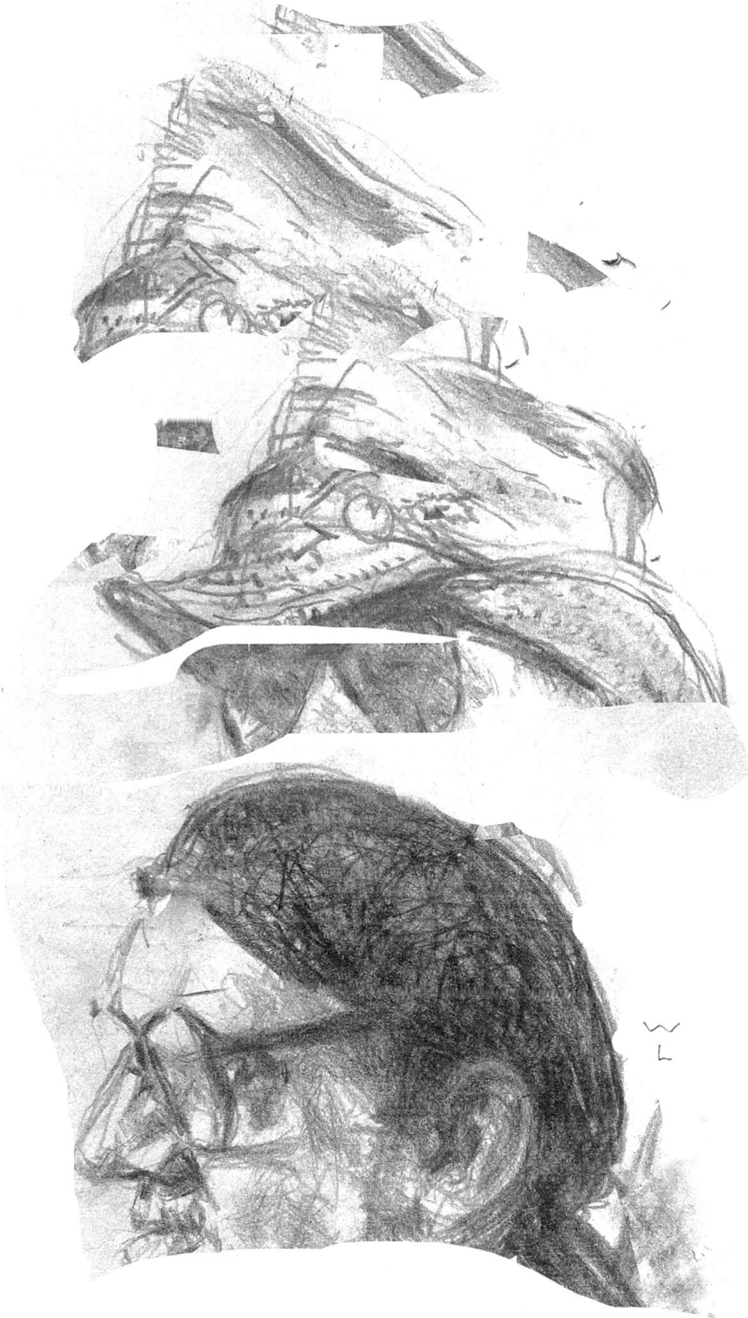

Jim had a gift for guiding others to peak performances. He once insisted that a band he was producing in New Orleans walk around outside and soak up the humidity to slow their frenetic playing. When Gregg Allman struggled to hit the right notes while recording "Midnight Rider," Jim supplied the joint that helped Allman settle into that song's mysterious sweet spot. He once told me he produced The Replacements record with his socks. He told stories, shared parables related to the task at hand, and riffed about recording the sound of molecules in the air.

It's the sort of thing that led Bill Bentley to write: "[Dickinson] has seen all that the world of music has to offer, and continues to believe that human beings playing instruments and singing songs hold the secrets of the universe. He also knows it is his job to help those musicians find a way to unlock the gifts hidden inside, and hopefully complete the delicate dance of capturing them for posterity."

WHEN GREGG ALLMAN STRUGGLED TO HIT THE RIGHT NOTES WHILE RECORDING "MIDNIGHT RIDER," JIM SUPPLIED THE JOINT THAT HELPED ALLMAN SETTLE INTO THAT SONG'S MYSTERIOUS SWEET SPOT.

Jim adhered to a production manifesto that reveals his approach to making records.

It reads:

> The unretainable nature of the present creates in Man a desire to capture the moment. Our fears of extinction compel us to record, to re-create, the ritual ceremony. From the first handprint cave painting to the most modern computer art, it is the human condition to seek immortality. Life is fleeting. Art is long. A record is a "totem," a document of a unique, unrepeatable event worthy of preservation and able to sustain historic life. The essence of the event is its soul.

He was a master at conjuring that soulful essence.

> Record production is a subtle, covert activity. The producer is an invisible man. His role remains a mystery. During the recording process there is an energy field present in the studio—to manipulate and to maximize that presence, to focus on the peculiar "harmony of the moment" is the job of the producer. Music has a spirit beyond the notes and rhythm. To foster that spirit and to cause it to flourish— to capture it at its peak—is the producer's task.

Jim's process did not involve yelling, kicking, or throwing things.

LIFE IS FLEETING

ART
IS

LONG

The call from Dylan came on January 13th, and Dickinson flew to Miami the next day. He headed straight to Victor Pianos and Organs on NW 54th Street, where he knew from his days with the Dixie Flyers that he could find an extensive selection of keyboards. Actually, Victor stocked a building full of grand pianos, a building of uprights, another building full of organs, and one of assorted keyboards. Jim picked out a Wurlitzer electric piano, a pump organ, and an old upright to be delivered to the studio.

Dickinson may have been the last musician through the door at Criteria, but he proved to be the final, and most important, piece of the puzzle. Once there, he found Dylan to be unusually focused and attentive to his muse, much like the artist he saw in *Don't Look Back*, D.A. Pennebaker's documentary of Dylan's 1965 U.K. tour. "The one thing that stood out in that film—in my mind, as shocking—was how professional Bob Dylan was," recalled Dickinson. "But why expect him not to be? On this session, one of the things I really enjoyed was the level of professionalism. It's very rewarding to see a support crew in place and everything working, a well-oiled machine, which he certainly has. . . .

> HE HEADED STRAIGHT TO VICTOR PIANOS AND ORGANS ON NW 54TH STREET, WHERE HE KNEW FROM HIS DAYS WITH THE DIXIE FLYERS THAT HE COULD FIND AN EXTENSIVE SELECTION OF KEYBOARDS.

W
L

Nobody was trying to look busy in front of the boss."

Dylan, like Chuck Berry, had a reputation for being difficult and aloof, but not so with Jim. "I played with Chuck Berry at the New Orleans music festival, and you hear horror stories about playing with Chuck Berry," said Dickinson. "He could not have been nicer to me, and everything was in the right key. Same thing with Bob Dylan."

It didn't take long for Dylan and Dickinson to establish a rapport. On a smoke break during Jim's first day at Criteria, Dylan suddenly appeared. "Hey, didn't you play with Sleepy John [Estes]?" he said playfully. He then asked Jim, who gigged with Estes, how the bluesman played a certain guitar lick.

Jim, possessing a font of arcane knowledge, passed along the secret: Estes made his G chord with one finger, instead of three. "If you do it any other way, it ain't gonna sound right," said Dickinson, who later mailed Dylan a video of Estes playing the part.

> **JIM, POSSESSING A FONT OF ARCANE KNOWLEDGE, PASSED ALONG THE SECRET: ESTES MADE HIS G CHORD WITH ONE FINGER, INSTEAD OF THREE. "IF YOU DO IT ANY OTHER WAY, IT AIN'T GONNA SOUND RIGHT."**

Dylan was fascinated by Memphis and its music history. "The last time I was [there]," he said, "I went to Humes, and they let me walk around in the halls."

Jim immediately understood the significance: Elvis Presley graduated from Humes High School in 1953. He also knew that the once all-white school was mostly African American at the time Dylan visited, and he must have been a surreal site walking around in his cowboy hat and pointed boots. Dylan said he found his way to the auditorium, where Presley gave one of his first public performances, singing Teresa Brewer's "'Till I Waltz Again with You" for a school talent show. He climbed the stage steps and gazed out over the room. Then, he looked down and spotted a lucky penny.

Jim was struck by the humanity, and humility, at the heart of the story. "That's the way I found being with him, human and really rewarding," he said. "It's just like Chuck Berry, man. If he wanted to be an asshole, he certainly has every right to be, to the world in general or to me personally. He has the right to do and say whatever the fuck he wants. To come off so human, when I've seen so many lesser people not even try. . . . Then [to mention], 'I found a lucky penny.' He didn't have to say that."

The moment was revelatory. "He's a person still in awe of Elvis, as well he should be, as everyone should be," noted Dickinson.

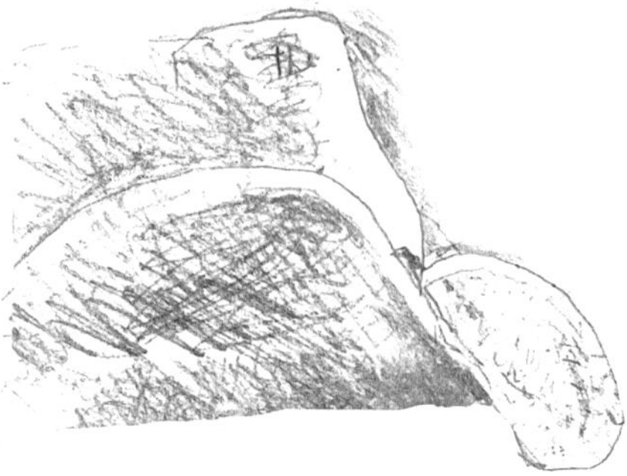

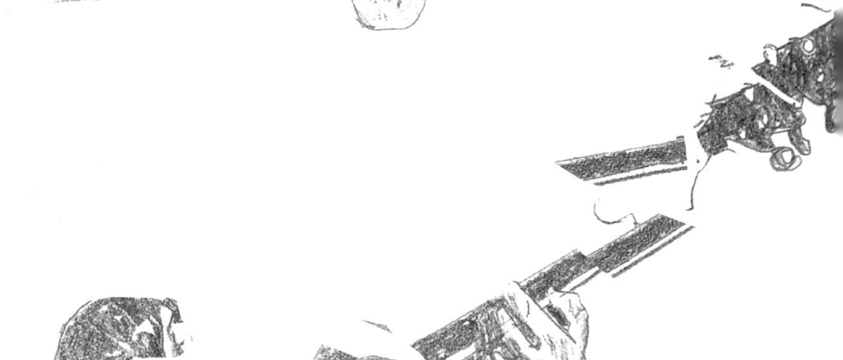

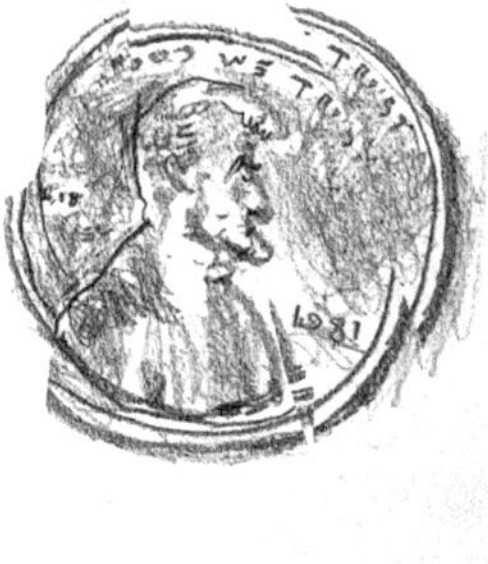
WE TRUST
1981

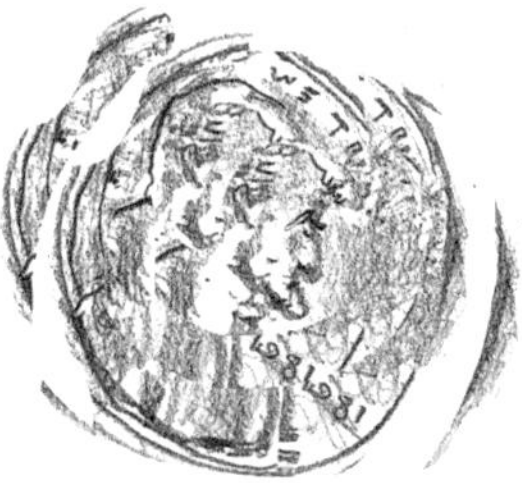

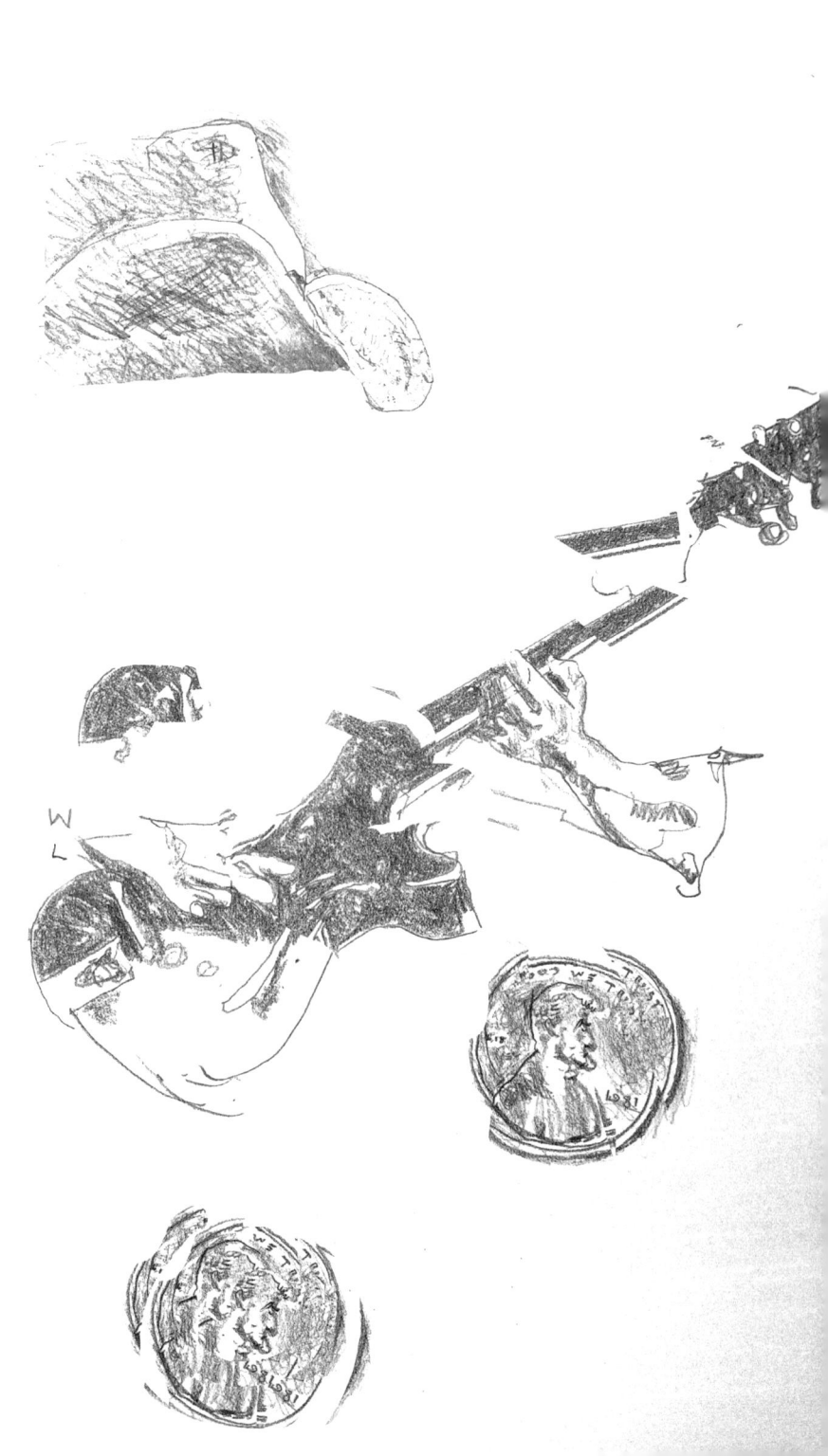

HE CLIMBED THE STAGE STEPS AND GAZED OUT OVER THE ROOM.
THEN, HE LOOKED DOWN AND SPOTTED A LUCKY PENNY.

IN THE PARKING LOT THAT FIRST EVENING AT CRITERIA, DYLAN AND DICKINSON MAY HAVE SEEN THE LIGHTS COME ON AT THE FUNERAL HOME NEXT DOOR. JIM RECALLED THE CLOUDS GLOWING PINK OVERHEAD, A NIGHTTIME PHENOMENON HE REMEMBERED FROM PREVIOUS SESSIONS IN MIAMI.

Dylan and Dickinson shared such awe because they remember what life was like before rock and roll, before Elvis Presley. Jim caught two Presley shows in Memphis in 1956. "Anyone who saw Elvis and said they were inspired to have a career in music is lying because seeing him was like seeing something that wasn't human," he recalled. "Nobody in their right mind could look at Elvis Presley and think that they could do what he was doing, because it was that strange. . . . Elvis just glowed."

When Dylan was discharged from the hospital after being treated for a potentially fatal heart ailment a few months before *Time Out of Mind*'s release, he quipped, "I really thought I'd be seeing Elvis soon." That wasn't long after his pilgrimage to Humes.

In the parking lot that first evening at Criteria, Dylan and Dickinson may have seen the lights come on at the funeral home next door. Jim recalled the clouds glowing pink overhead, a nighttime phenomenon he remembered from previous sessions in Miami.

When they got back to work, I'm betting Dylan sensed he'd gained an ally, someone who shared his perspective. He could trust Jim.

The roadie who met Dickinson at the airport informed him there were a dozen musicians on the session. Jim assumed they were on-call, adding parts as needed. Instead, he found the entire group playing together: three drummers, two pedal steel guitarists, three electric guitarists (including Lanois), a bassist, keyboard player, and Dylan.

"When I say there were three drum kits, I mean there were three drum kits playing simultaneously," said Dickinson. "There were never less than two drums and percussion, and the two steel guitars playing simultaneously, which I've never even heard before on a country session. . . . There were definitely two bands there and two agendas. Lanois had a band and Dylan had a band, and there was a good deal of tension resulting from that."

Of the musicians, Dickinson knew Keltner well—they'd played together on various Ry Cooder sessions. So he set up his keyboards near Keltner's drums, where he had an unobstructed view of Dylan singing. Because Dylan had a concert grand of his own, Dickinson gravitated towards the electric piano he'd rented. He figured that, in order to be heard, he needed to craft a distinctive sound, rather than play a lot of notes, so he turned up the vibrato. "I thought Dylan had me there to lay down a groove," said Dickinson.

The studio tapes from Jim's first day—the session sheets identified him as the "whirly" on track 20—reveal that's exactly what happened. After Dickinson sat down at the Wurlitzer and got a feel for the instrument, the band launched into "Can't Wait." As Dickinson started to play, Dylan murmured, "Yeah," which was notable, because, on the hundreds of tapes I listened to in Tulsa, it was the only time I heard him encourage one of the players. Twenty seconds later, it happened again: "Yeah," repeated Dylan, this time a little louder.

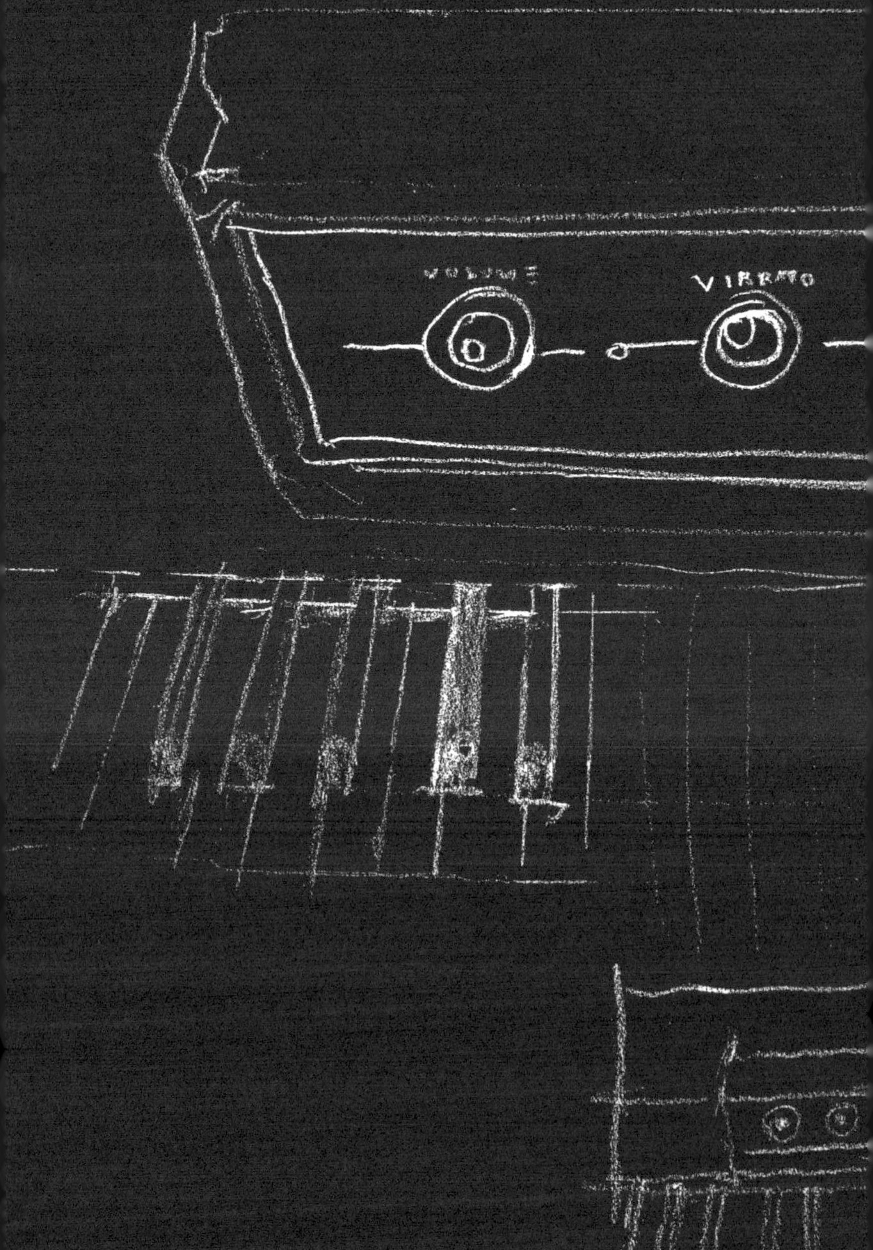
VOLUME
VIBRATO

THE SESSION SHEETS IDENTIFIED HIM AS THE "WHIRLY" ON TRACK 20

Jim generated a churning groove, thick and deep. As it swelled, it pulled the guitars and drums along with it, and Dylan growled lyrics about burning air and struggling to think straight. A minute later, guitar strings resonated at peculiar frequencies with sturdy dissonance that fortified lines like: "Skies are grey, I'm lookin' for anything that'll bring a happy glow/Night or day, it doesn't matter where I go anymore I just go."

The two bands pushed and pulled, struggling for dominance and threatening a collapse that only heightened the tension in Dylan's conflicted lyrics. After he sang a final "don't know how much longer I can wait" at the six-minute mark, the Wurlitzer rumbled mightily and a barely-controlled chaos ensued, the session-vet guitarists dropped all pretext of perfection, and the entire ensemble played with primal intensity. Their clashing chords whipped up whirling overtones that continued for another blissful minute. After the surge receded, a lone pedal steel punctuated it all with a few pristine notes that, if anything, underscored the song's transformation over the previous seven-and-a-half minutes.

More than simply a departure, this Dickinson take shed layers of accumulated affectation. Everyone exuded more energy and swagger, and Dylan finally sounded like he wasn't chasing a trend or some past glory. Instead, he was getting personal *and* getting outside himself, confronting mortality and tapping into some mythic and mystical realm he'd abandoned, or maybe believed had abandoned him.

The overall vibe brought to mind Dickinson's description of his own recordings, evoking "Ghost art, a sine wave of memory. Tales of outlaws, train wrecks, lost love, heroic death, manly valor, prayer. A mad street preacher's sermon. Picture a drunken circus band staggering down a winding country road. Down in the bottom where the bullfrog gets his water."

The Dickinson version of "Can't Wait" was dubbed the "funk" take in the session documents. The standard definitions of that word apply, especially considering the direction *Time Out of*

> THE OVERALL VIBE BROUGHT TO MIND
> DICKINSON'S DESCRIPTION OF HIS OWN
> RECORDINGS, EVOKING "GHOST ART,
> A SINE WAVE OF MEMORY. TALES OF
> OUTLAWS, TRAIN WRECKS, LOST LOVE,
> HEROIC DEATH, MANLY VALOR, PRAYER."

Mind would take. Funk, noun: 1. A state of depression. 2. A style of popular dance music based on elements of blues and soul. 3. A strong musty smell of sweat or tobacco. Early 17th century: to blow smoke on.

Dickinson, who considered himself "the enemy of institutional order," quashed any notion of Dylan making an alternative-radio-friendly record, *Blonde on Blonde* 2.0, or some toothless psychedelia. He accompanied Dylan down a road less traveled that proved more singular than desolate.

The following week was productive. "Not Dark Yet" and "Dirt Road Blues" gritted gloriously and thickened with possibility. The songs demanded feeling, not flash, and that's what Dickinson provided with his ghosted, blues drenched grooves. Engineer Mark Howard recalled that Dylan sometimes refused to play piano, because "Bob wanted [Dickinson's] vibe on it."

Dickinson certainly felt that was the case. "I don't think [Dylan] wanted to hear me," he said. "I think he wanted to feel me."

Dickinson believed Dylan had scrutinized his work with Ry Cooder and understood how that vibe infused Cooder's evocative soundtracks, especially *Paris, Texas* and *The Border*. Dylan was definitely familiar with that material and was known to perform "Across the Borderline," a song Dickinson co-wrote for the latter film. Jim penned the key verse:

**HE ACCOMPANIED DYLAN
DOWN A ROAD LESS TRAVELED
THAT PROVED MORE
SINGULAR THAN DESOLATE.**

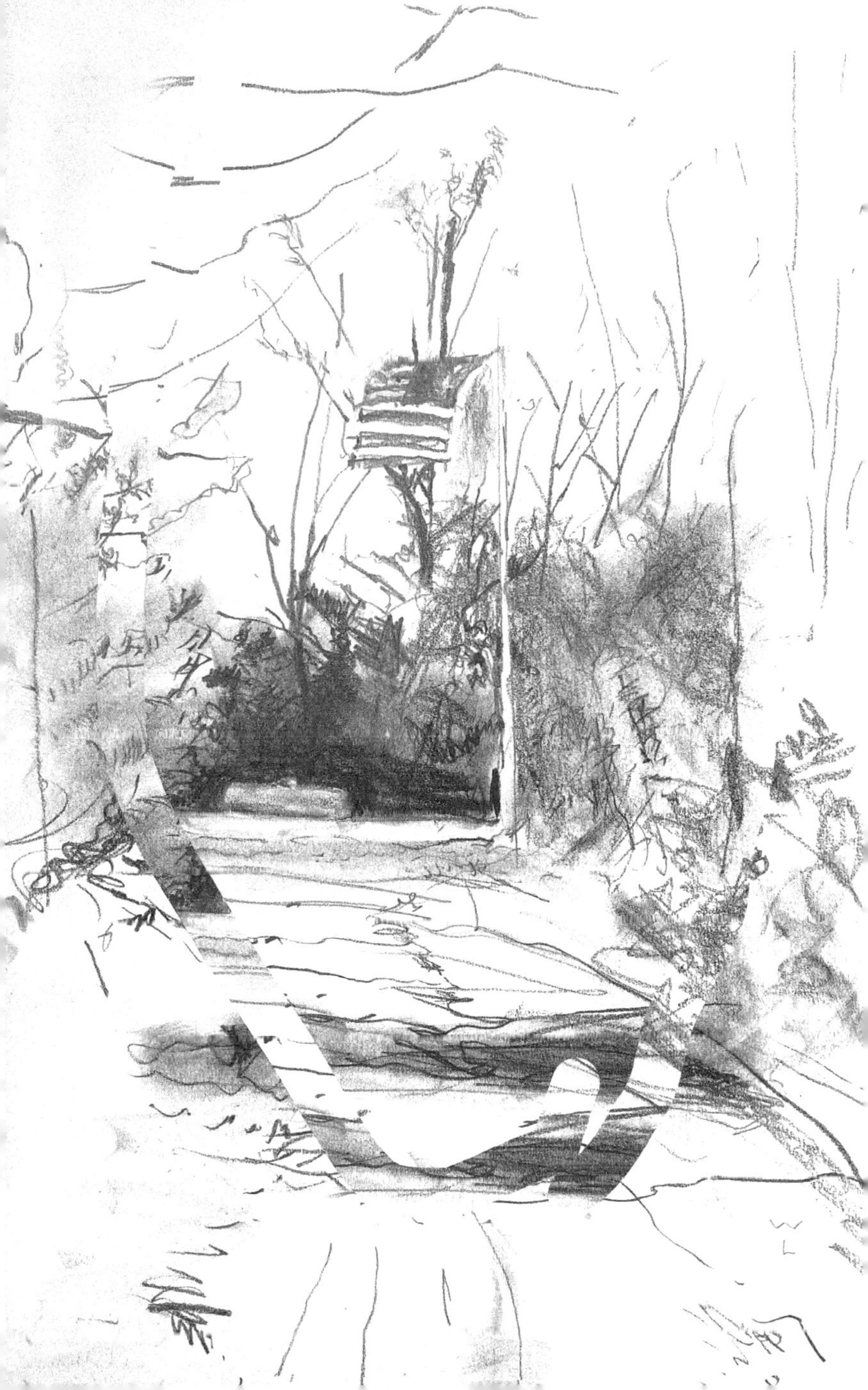

> Up and down the Rio Grande
> A thousand footprints in the sand
> Reveal a secret no one can define
> That river rolls on like a breath
> In between my life and death
> Tell me, who is next to cross that borderline

Dylan knew that the man who wrote those lines would understand what *Time Out of Mind* was all about. [When the song became the title track of Willie Nelson's *Across the Borderline* album, Jim said he'd use the royalties to have his driveway repaved. He wasn't kidding.]

If every tune didn't realize its full potential, it wasn't Jim's fault. While working on "Girl from the Red River Shore," for instance, Dylan quipped that they'd need a string section to take it any further. Lanois told him it couldn't be done. "Had I been Lanois, I would have started calling symphony players," said Dickinson. "What do you mean we can't do that? We'll do that tomorrow. Tonight would be even better. Think about what Van Dyke Parks could do writing an arrangement for a Bob Dylan song. You'd be talking about Aaron Copland or something." The song was, ultimately, left off the album.

Dickinson would have gone through the trouble, he said, because the song seemed important to Dylan. "If you heard somebody sing ['Girl from the Red River Shore'] right after 'Oh Susannah,' you would completely buy it," he said. "I don't mean that in any demeaning fashion. Read the lyrics to 'Oh Susannah' and tell me it's not some deep shit. . . .This was the same use of the language, which, god knows, is what [Dylan] is a genius at."

> "LISTENING BACK TO IT, IT'S LIKE YOU'RE ALONE IN THE ROOM WITH HIM. IT'S AN INTIMATE, OPEN-SOUL DELIVERY, AN ATTEMPT TO COMMUNICATE AND NOT BE VAGUE."

Dylan frequently revised his lyrics on a notepad in the studio and sang the new songs with such depth and emotion "it was almost embarrassing," recalled Dickinson. "Listening back to it, it's like you're alone in the room with him. It's an intimate, open-soul delivery, an attempt to communicate and not be vague."

Dylan told Jim he'd been working on some of them for a couple of years. The notes Dylan kept prior to the sessions are archived in Tulsa, and they shed light on his mindset at the time. On Mayfair Hotel stationary, he jotted, "It's too late to change your life," "everything going to the dogs," and "I turn my back to the wall as [the parade] passes by." A portion of that last line would turn up in an early draft of "Can't Wait."

His cramped scrawls on Hotel Copenhagen notepaper included: "the fat is in the fire" and "if it's all as hollow as it seems." The former turned up in "Cold Irons Bound," and the latter found its way into the final verse of "Tryin' to Get to Heaven." He jotted down "hearts, a-thumpin'," which he changed to "hearts a-beatin'" in the fifth verse of "Heaven." And his written reminder to "walk around and work" foretold wanderings through Boston and Cambridge in "Highlands."

The writing on the back of a fax dated March 4, 1996 included the following phrases: "punishing each other," "feed off each other's pain," "the holy people live without a code," "time rages onward," and "everything I know is wrong." There was also a glimmer of hope, as Dylan hinted at a forward path, a way out of the malaise gripping him: "when the roads were impassable," he wrote, "trumpets are sounding."

He also felt the need to remind himself of "the most dangerous place of all, the middle of the road." It echoed Neil Young's *Decade* liner notes, where Young wrote that the massive success of "Heart of Gold" landed him "in the middle of the road. Traveling there soon became a bore so I headed for the ditch."

The reference gives new meaning, perhaps, to the "I'm listening to Neil Young" line in "Highlands," bending it from album listening to advice taking. But maybe not: on an earlier draft, Dylan was listening to Charlie Parker.

Jim firmly believed the lyrics dictated *Time Out of Mind* should be a blues album. Bleak, resilient, and shrouded in mystery, they exhibited a sort of steely endurance in the face of existential crisis. "The lyrics may be coming from a dark place," said Dickinson, "but the fucking record is about

> "THERE WOULD BE LONG PERIODS OF CHAOS AND THEN TEN MINUTES, MAYBE LESS, OF CLARITY WHERE EVERYTHING CAME TOGETHER, EVERYBODY GOT OUT OF THE WAY, AND IT HAPPENED."

survival. He is a blues singer, the real deal, and this is important music."

Lanois felt differently. He wondered aloud if they were cutting too many blues songs and told Mark Howard he "didn't want to make another blues record." He also told Dickinson and Keltner he was uncomfortable with how things were going at Criteria. "Lanois verbalized it at several points," said Dickinson. "He said, 'This is not the way I do things.'"

Lanois, a studio geek, was accustomed to controlled environments, not the sprawling and spontaneous sessions that unfolded at Criteria. Dylan's approach brought to mind Miles Davis's electric period, when Davis assembled large ensembles that ventured into the unknown with unruly, often thrilling, results. "When it worked, it was amazing," Dickinson said. "There would be long periods of chaos and then ten minutes, maybe less, of clarity where everything came together, everybody got out of the way, and it happened."

It's likely why Dylan and Lanois reached a breaking point. According to Howard, "The energy in the studio had become weird," so weird that Dylan sometimes ignored Lanois completely. One day, Dylan and Howard were mixing a track, and Lanois told them he liked what they were doing. Dylan turned to Howard and asked, "Do you hear someone talking?"

Howard simply replied, "No."

Dylan, while icing out Lanois, started seeking another opinion. With the band gathered in the control room one night, Dylan asked during a playback, "What do you think about that, Jim?" Jim Keltner—who'd worked with Dylan on *Shot of Love*, *Saved*, and *The 30th Anniversary Concert Celebration*—started to respond, but Dylan interrupted: "No, I mean him," he said and pointed to Dickinson.

Dylan sought Jim's feedback so often that Dickinson felt compelled to visit Lanois at his hotel and apologize. He'd

"THE MOST DANGEROUS PLACE OF ALL,

THE MIDDLE OF THE ROAD."

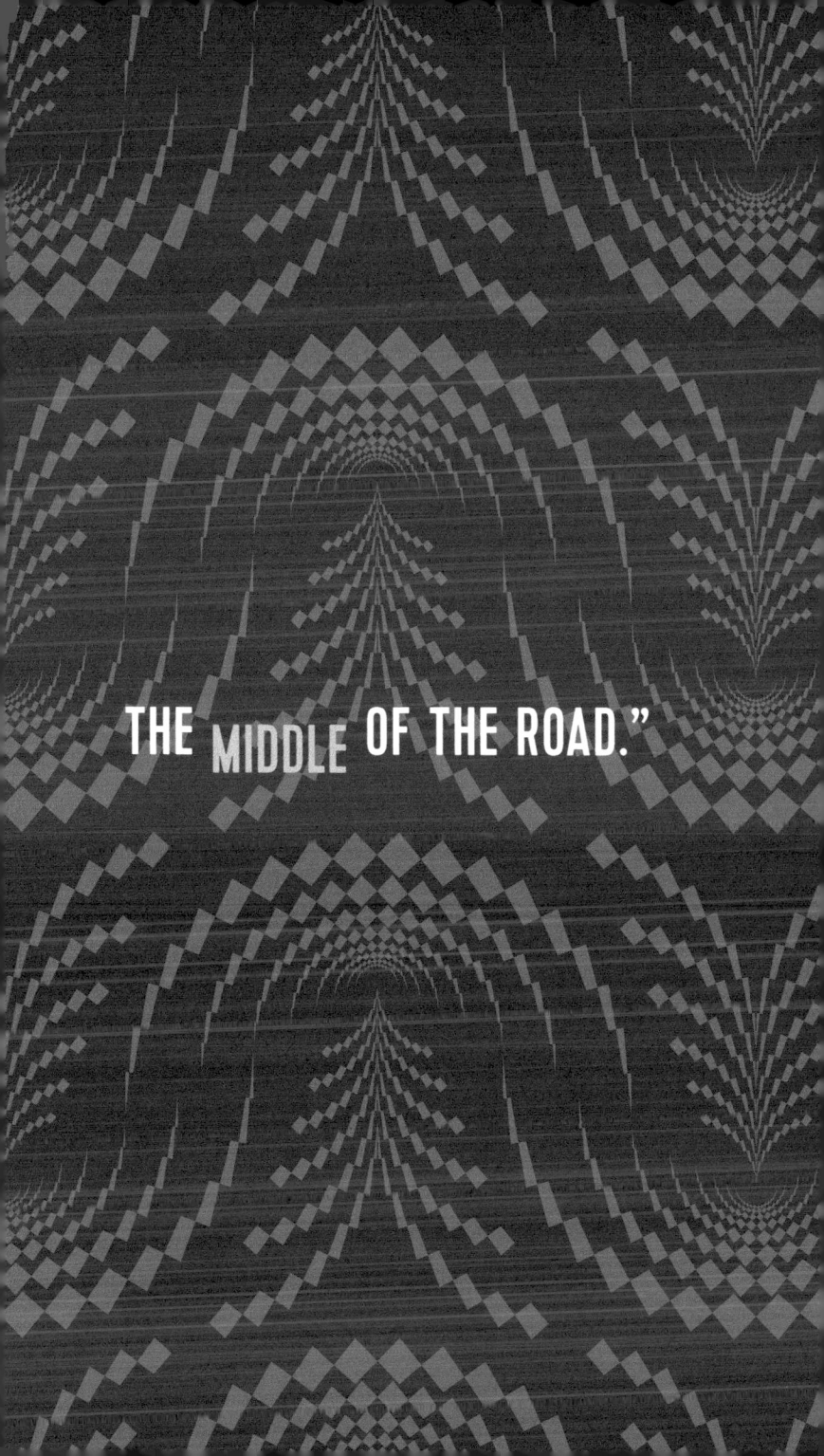

> "BY REPUTATION, I WILL SAY WHAT I MEAN," SAID DICKINSON, "AND I WILL SAY SHIT THAT PEOPLE FROM LOS ANGELES WON'T SAY."

produced enough records to understand that—in this scenario, as a session player—he was stepping on Lanois's toes. Still, he told Lanois: "If [Dylan] asks me [something], I'm gonna tell him."

According to Howard, Lanois was eventually banished from the control room and forced to work on mixes in an adjacent room. "Dylan wouldn't talk to him," recalled Howard, "so [Lanois] would have to come to me and tell me what to say to Dylan."

Dickinson had Dylan's ear at this critical juncture. "By reputation, I will say what I mean," said Dickinson, "and I will say shit that people from Los Angeles won't say. It's exactly what you're not supposed to do."

And what was he telling Dylan? "I told him what I would have said if I was producing the session. If we had three or four cuts, for instance, he'd ask me which one I liked. Not always specific, mostly producer shit."

It continued through Jim's last day at Criteria, January 21st.

After Dickinson returned home, he got to thinking about what happened in Miami. Dylan brought him in to lay down a groove, that was certain, but any number of musicians might have played that role. No, he was there for other reasons, as well.

Then, it dawned on him: "[Dylan] had me there as a counterbalance. I was there to produce Lanois."

Dickinson told me a few times that, over the course of his career, some things were disappointing, but working so closely with Dylan was not one of them. "The obvious comparison in my career is the Stones," he said, "but it was so far beyond the Stones that that's not valid. The only thing I can compare it to in my experience is Little Richard. That's a weird thing to say, but Little Richard had the same kind of total star quality. When he walked into the room, the room changed."

Such a powerful presence would intimidate many people, but Jim was nonplussed. Unimpressed by celebrity, he connected artistically and personally to Dylan and appreciated his creative process. "I never saw the uncomfortable artist," said Dickinson. "The results he got at Criteria were so overwhelming that you could see he was pleased. It was a beautiful thing to see somebody working so well at what they do."

Jim lauded his fellow musicians for rising to the occasion. "We were able to match the material's emotional depth and understanding of life," he said. "For want of a better word, there was an age group present. It was heroic. It was heroic for all of us. You're there to rob the train, the bank, or whatever the job is. That's what we did."

He speculated about how the album would sound relative to what he heard at Criteria. He explained that, as they were recording, the headphone mix "sounded like shit." Dickinson opted, like Dylan, to forego headphones in order to hear what was happening in the room, which sounded different. And the playbacks were different still. "I think about music visually," Jim said, "and this was like a Diego Rivera mural. It was real big and real broad and very encompassing. Like with a mural, you could look at any piece of it and see a whole picture. That's the way this was."

As a result, the material could be mixed any number of ways. "God only knows how the finished record will sound," he wondered.

"LIKE WITH A MURAL, YOU COULD LOOK AT ANY PIECE OF IT AND SEE A WHOLE PICTURE. THAT'S THE WAY THIS WAS."

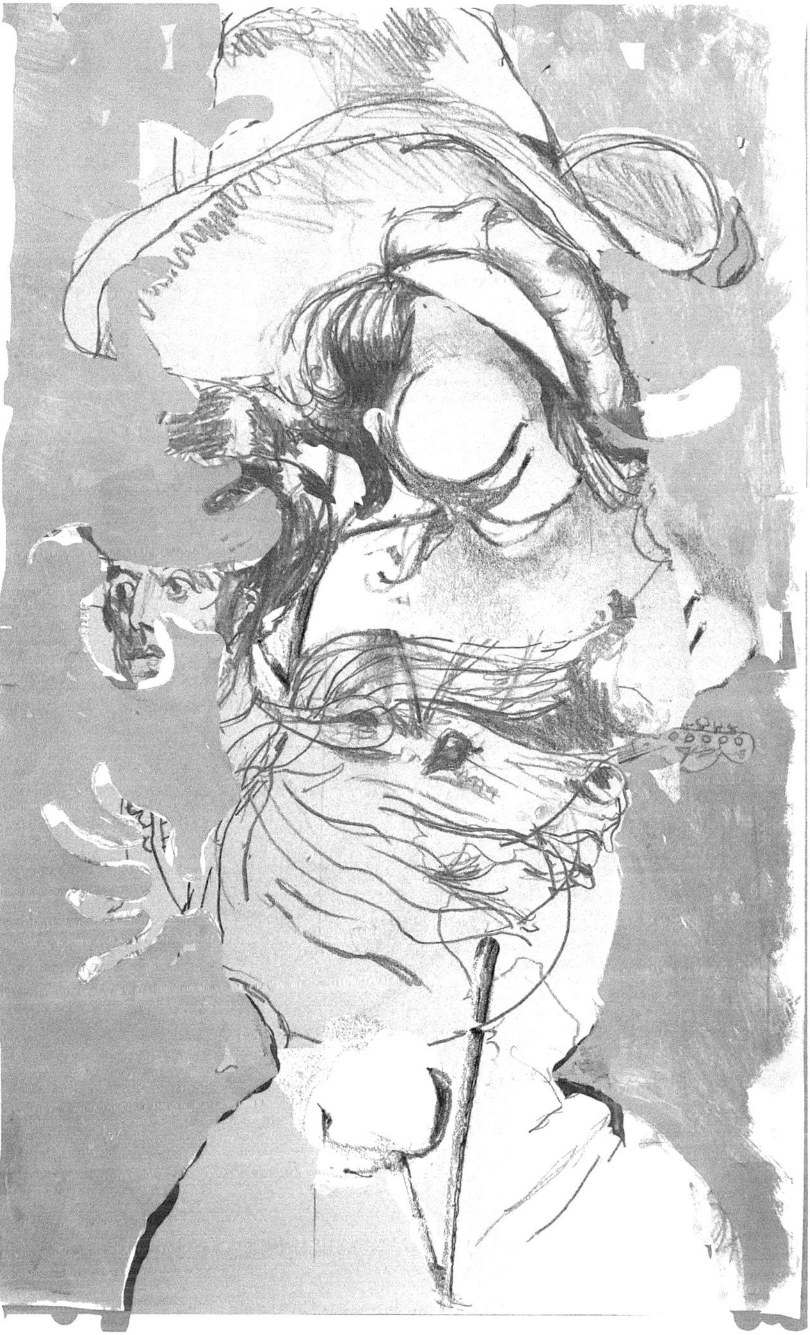

I said I wished he was producing it, and Jim defended Lanois. In fact, he claimed to have admired his work for years and had studied some of his production techniques. Still, he would have welcomed a role in post-production. "I wish I was mixing it, I'll tell you that," he said, believing it would be a classic Dylan record "if it survives intact." [Note: In March 2016, *Rolling Stone* reported that an archive curator had come across "a completely different version of *Time Out of Mind* produced by pianist Jim Dickinson." An update of the article later stated, "Dickinson denies such a thing exists," which was curious considering the fact that Jim had been dead for six years prior to his supposed denial.]

The finished record was, indeed, special, and Columbia Records President Don Ienner knew it. In a letter dated May 14, 1997, Ienner wrote to Dylan: "I just wanted to tell you how thrilled I am by your new album. The more time I get to spend with it, the more impressed I am by the level of songwriting and performance." Ienner gushed that "the album exceeds all our expectations" and anticipated it having "a profound impact," because of songs such as "Not Dark Yet," "Gotta Get to Heaven" (later renamed "Tryin' to Get to Heaven"), "Highlands," and "Make You Feel My Love."

He stated the need to map out a release strategy that will "focus on the level of its achievement" and settle on a release date no later than September to be eligible for Grammy consideration. "I couldn't be more excited," Ienner concluded. "[I'm] looking forward to seeing this album get the attention and acclaim it deserves."

Columbia released *Time Out of Mind*, Dylan's 30th studio album, on September 30, 1997. As Dickinson suspected and Ienner predicted, it generated a great deal of acclaim:

> The album is far and away Dylan's best sustained work since the mid-1970's; it reaches the exalted level of *Blood on the Tracks*. (*The New York Times*)

"This album is **far and away** Dylan's **best sustained work** since the mid-1970's; it reaches the **exalted level** of *Blood on the Tracks*."

{ *THE NEW YORK TIMES* }

> This haunting masterpiece rivals the peaks in Dylan's rich and varied catalog attesting to the creative renaissance of an artist still bent on defying expectations and spurning trends. (*USA Today*)
>
> The rumor is true: Bob Dylan, an artist for whom many fans had simply given up hope, has made an excellent album. Dylan's first collection of new songs in six years, *Time Out Of Mind* is a stark, haunted work that recalls his best material and doesn't suffer by comparison. *Time Out Of Mind* should remind old fans why Dylan used to be called a genius on a regular basis, and could convince some new ones that it was a title fittingly bestowed. (*A.V. Club*)
>
> [Dylan] hasn't sounded so fresh and almighty in years. It's enough to give us some faith in the future. (*Newsweek*)
>
> He's making some of the best music of his life. (*The Chicago Tribune*)

Rolling Stone, in its four-star review, cited Dickinson for crafting "hypnotic, steady-rolling grooves that suggest a spooky David Lynch soundtrack. The empathetic, low-key support flatters Dylan's increasingly pinched voice to far greater effect than he has received on many of his recordings of the last 15 years."

In my November 13th *New Times* review, I lauded the record's "sparse, spooky vibe" for enhancing the gravitas of Dylan's lyrics and called *Time Out of Mind* a "masterpiece."

It proved to be a commercial smash, too, becoming Dylan's first Top Ten record since *Slow Train Coming* in 1979. It sold more than a million copies and was certified platinum.

Dickinson was impressed with how the record showcased Dylan's creative abilities. "Growth is a remarkable thing for an artist as developed as Dylan is, especially when it'd be so easy to go back to the past," he said. "It brings to mind what I always tell my boys: 'Play every note like it's your last one, because one of them will be.'"

> "PLAY EVERY NOTE LIKE IT'S YOUR LAST ONE, BECAUSE ONE OF THEM WILL BE."

The first 30 seconds of *Time Out of Mind* function as a statement of intent. They set the tone for not only the opening song ("Love Sick") but also the entire album. Augie Meyers, at the outset, repeats a solitary chord on the organ, as Dylan sings, "I'm walkin' through streets that are dead," in a ravaged voice. It's stark, startling and delivered with beady-eyed focus. It doesn't stake a claim that the old Dylan is back so much as it announces that Dylan is old, and has something new to say.

I literally turned and looked at my speakers the first time I heard it. Reading *Chronicles*, I'd think back to that moment, as Dylan recalled hearing Robert Johnson for the first time:

> From the first note the vibrations from the loudspeaker made my hair stand up. The stabbing sounds from the guitar could almost break a window. When Johnson started singing, he seemed like a guy who could have sprung from the head of Zeus in full armor.

That's how I felt listening to "Love Sick."

Dylan and Lanois deserve credit for pushing the vocals far up in the mix to make an immediate impression. It vaults Dylan into the company of Johnson and Howlin' Wolf and suggests *Time Out of Mind* will be a compelling listen in the vein of mid-to-late-period triumphs by Billie Holiday, Miles Davis, or Glenn Gould. [How is it that all these artists, including Dylan, recorded for Columbia?]

IT DOESN'T
STAKE A CLAIM
THAT THE OLD
DYLAN IS BACK
SO MUCH AS
IT ANNOUNCES
THAT DYLAN IS
OLD, AND HAS
SOMETHING
NEW TO SAY.

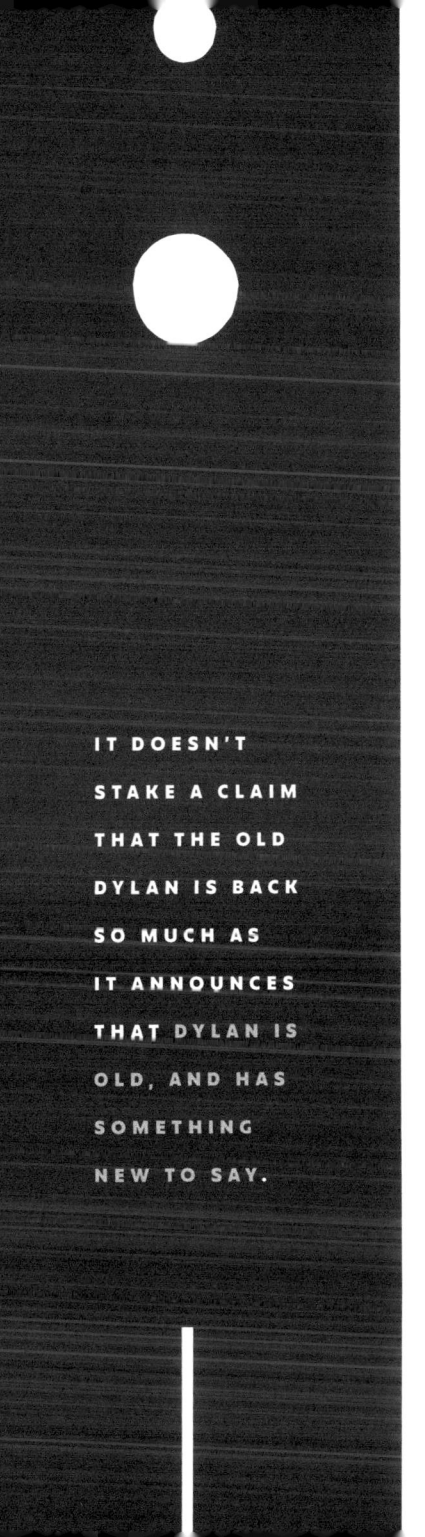

The record unfolds with robust momentum. A fractured rockabilly vibe propels "Dirt Road Blues" forward as it nods to the past. "Standing in the Doorway" downshifts to a crawl as Dylan laments that "yesterday everything was goin' too fast/today it's movin' too slow" and segues into the sweltering swing of "Million Miles" and its distance-between-us lament. "Tryin' to Get to Heaven" broadens the distance geographically and historically, as Dylan steps back in time, claims to have fled Missouri (with stops in Baltimore and New Orleans), and knows plenty of people who'd put him up for a day or two. He travels by train, steamboat, and horse-and-buggy, but, ultimately, he's "tryin' to get to heaven" and yearning for transcendence.

The next five songs comprise the heart of the album. "'Til I Fell in Love with You" and "Can't Wait" swagger with gusto, thanks to Dickinson's groove.

W
L

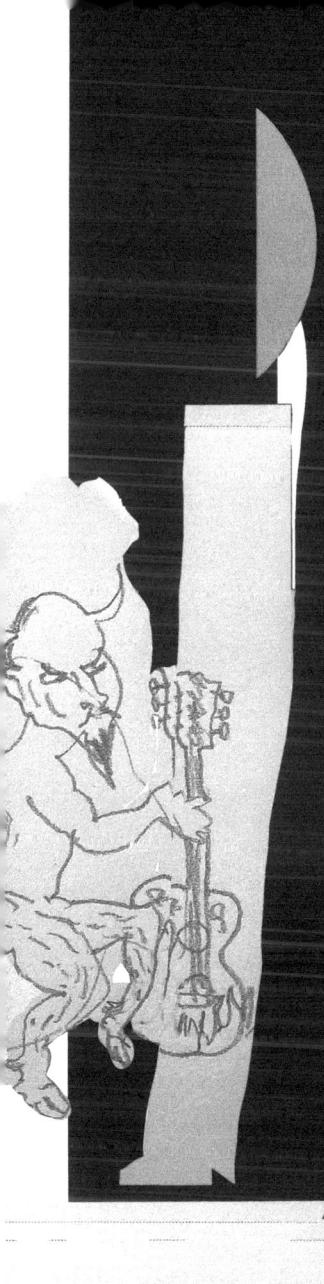

TRYIN'
TO
GET
TO
HEAVEN

You'd never know "Can't Wait" was so problematic, because the finished version crackles with energy. Side by side, "Cold Irons Bound" and "Make You Feel My Love" contrast dramatically, as the former roars through a litany of psychic torments and the latter pledges allegiance and reassurance. It may be tempting to dismiss "Make You Feel My Love" as mere sentimentality—Billy Joel, Adele, Garth Brooks, and the cast of *Glee* would all cover the song—but, here, it shines valiantly, a chivalrous prompt that's both unexpected and welcome.

"Not Dark Yet" is the centerpiece of *Time Out of Mind*, an instant classic in the vein of "Every Grain of Sand." It thrums into existence, girded by funereal drums and quivering organ, as Dylan sings, "shadows are fallin' and I been here all day/it's too hot to sleep and time is runnin' away" with stately poise. He deftly navigates the space between personal pain and existential crisis, singing "there's not even room enough to be anywhere," "sometimes my

> **ONCE DYLAN DISCARDED ALL THE CLUTTER AND ALLOWED THE SONG TO SETTLE INTO THAT GHOSTED GROOVE, HE UNLOCKED ITS INHERENT POWER AND UNDERSTATED GRACE, WITHOUT SACRIFICING ANY OF ITS EVOCATIVE, MELANCHOLIC TONE. IT BECAME A THING OF TRUE BEAUTY.**

burden is more than I can bear," and "don't even hear the murmur of a prayer," before returning to "it's not dark yet, but it's getting there."

It speaks to Dylan's genius and intuition that the song evolved to this point. He had to fight for it, because, as the session tapes show, Lanois pushed other agendas and pushed hard: there was the Teatro gospel version, the "it's not dark yet, Danny boy" take, and the beat-driven attempts that confounded Dylan. Once Dylan discarded all the clutter and allowed the song to settle into that ghosted groove, he unlocked its inherent power and understated grace, without sacrificing any of its evocative, melancholic tone. It became a thing of true beauty.

"Highlands" closes the album with a flourish. It rambles and roams for 17 verses and no chorus, as Dylan meanders through the streets of Boston and the recesses of his mind. Nods to poets and pop culture figures mingle with flashes of humor and regret. Who but Dylan could reference Neil Young, Erica Jong, and Robert Burns in the same song?

WHO BUT DYLAN COULD REFERENCE NEIL YOUNG, ERICA JONG, AND ROBERT BURNS IN THE SAME SONG?

WL

At one point, he ducks into a restaurant and banters with a waitress. The Jong reference drops as a punch line that caps their exchange, but the set-up is more revealing: she challenges his cultural perspective ("You don't read women authors do ya?") and insists on being seen authentically ("That don't look a thing like me," she scoffs at his sketch). Though Dylan appears to win this round of one-upmanship with the "I've read Erica Jong" quip, he slips out the door when she isn't looking, which is hardly a victor's move. Like the rest of the record, it's an acknowledgement that the times have, indeed, changed.

He returns to the busy street, envying the young people he sees and wondering, drolly, if buying a full-length leather coat might ease his woes. It's a welcome note of levity, and the album winds down with these parting words, a glimmer of hope:

> Well my heart's in The Highlands at the break of day
> Over the hills and far away
> There's a way to get there, and I'll figure it out somehow
> Well I'm already there in my mind and that's good enough for now

From the outset, I loved the entire record and, unlike some others, didn't consider its overall sound or Lanois's production to be problematic or oppressive. But I had no idea, until my week in Tulsa, just how fraught the process of completing it had been.

Jim had mixed feelings about the released version. Though he never doubted *Time Out of Mind*'s achievement, he felt that "so much of it isn't there" and lamented the fact that two of his favorite songs, "Mississippi" and "Girl from the Red River Shore," didn't make the final cut. He explained that what he heard on the studio floor at Criteria wasn't what he heard on the finished album. In fact, much of what he experienced wasn't audible at all.

It reminded me of a parable Jim often repeated when talking about the creative process and a finished product. It basically goes like this: Imagine an Indian carving a totem pole, alone, in the middle of a forest. A thunderstorm comes up, but he keeps working despite the wind, rain, and lightning. He rides out the storm, finishes the pole, and leaves. Time passes and he returns with a friend to show him the carving. The friend likes it and says, "Good job." But the Indian is disappointed in what he sees, because he remembers, and longs for, the thunderstorm.

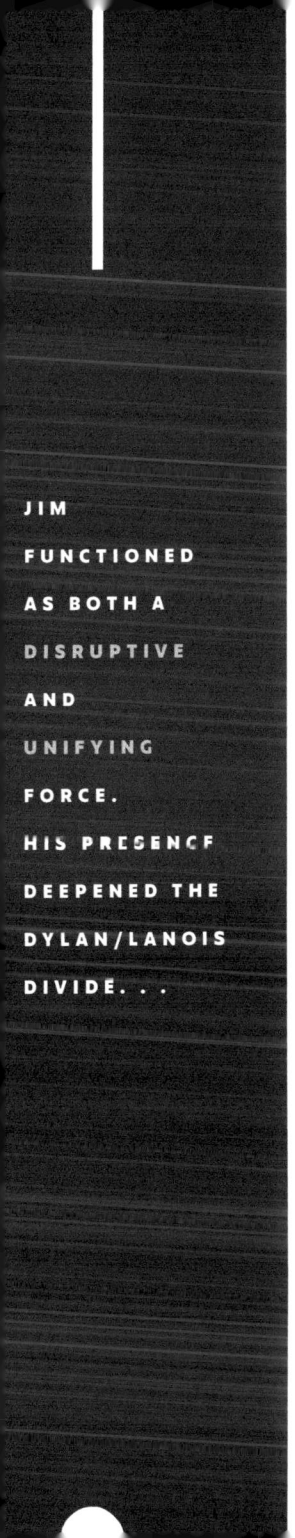

The exhilarating stretches at Criteria—when the band searched and probed before hitting a sweet spot that, Jim recalled, "was on the edge, distorted, and pulsating off the beat"—never made it to the album. The closest thing I heard to what Jim described was the "funk" version of "Can't Wait," recorded soon after his arrival in Miami. Jim had no way of knowing that what he conjured, over the course of those seven-and-a-half minutes, was the pivot point in the *Time Out of Mind* sessions. He wasn't privy to all the misdirection, conflict, and false starts that came before (though Keltner likely told him about some of it), but the tapes in Tulsa confirm that he significantly altered elements of particular songs as well as the overall vibe of the album.

Jim functioned as both a disruptive and unifying force. His presence deepened the Dylan/Lanois divide; Jim filled it with ghosted music and mythic mysteries that helped reconnect Dylan to essential truths that eluded him for so long. Dylan has sounded different, reinvigorated, ever since the "whirly" gig.

> JIM FUNCTIONED AS BOTH A DISRUPTIVE AND UNIFYING FORCE. HIS PRESENCE DEEPENED THE DYLAN/LANOIS DIVIDE...

WHIRLY GIG

T*ime Out of Mind* won "Album of the Year" at the 1998 Grammy Awards, and Dylan thanked Jim when accepting the award. In fact, he referred to him as "my brother from down in Mississippi." He also riffed about Robert Johnson's influence and the profundity of seeing Buddy Holly in concert, touchstones I could imagine him sharing with Jim during smoke breaks at Criteria.

Dylan thanked Lanois for his "help" producing the record.

Soon after the Grammys, Jim sent me a photograph taken in Miami. It seemed like a nifty souvenir at the time, but it's taken on added significance since my trip to Tulsa. It's a small black-and-white snapshot with Dylan in the foreground, instantly recognizable with cocked eyebrow and tousled hair. Lanois stands behind Dylan, over his left shoulder, wearing a black leather cap and flannel shirt.

There's a third person in the photo, too. He's positioned behind Lanois, furthest from the camera, and slightly out of focus.

It's Jim, looking like he has Dylan's back. ◆

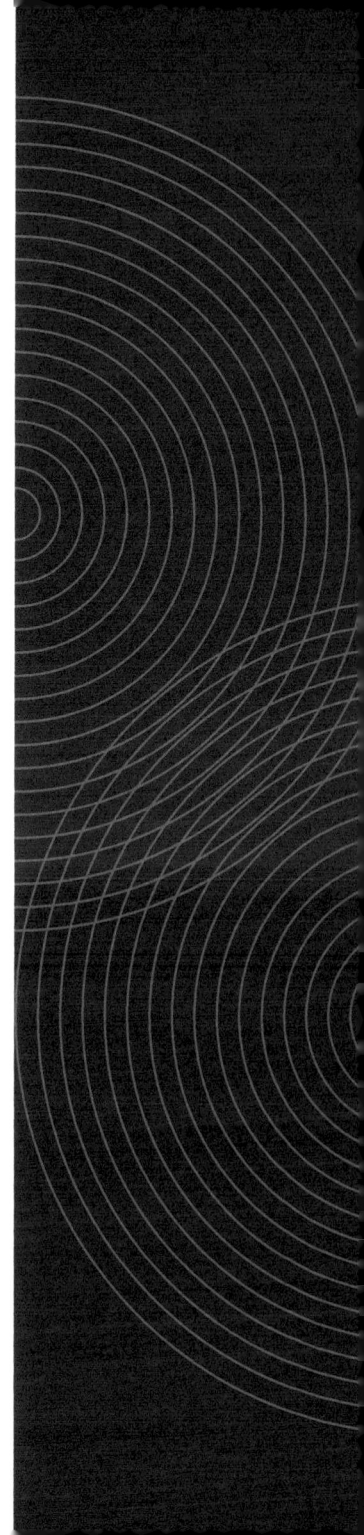

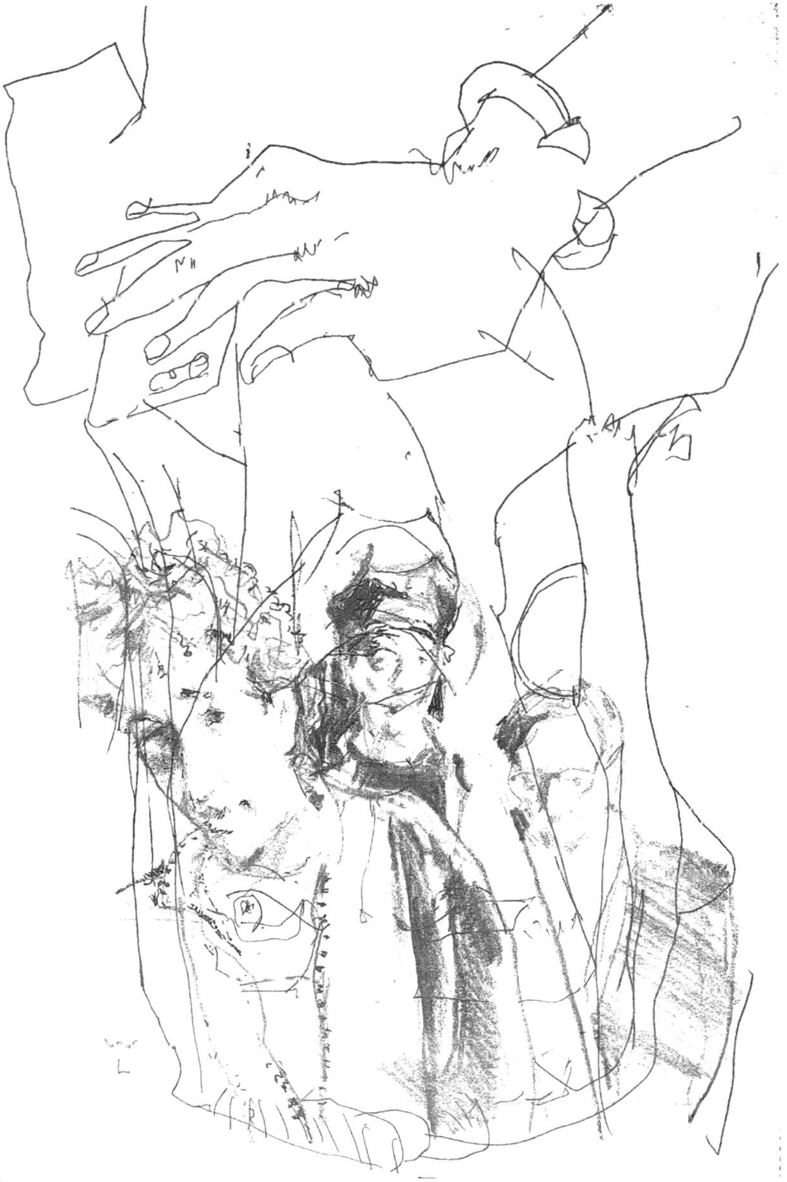

THE END.

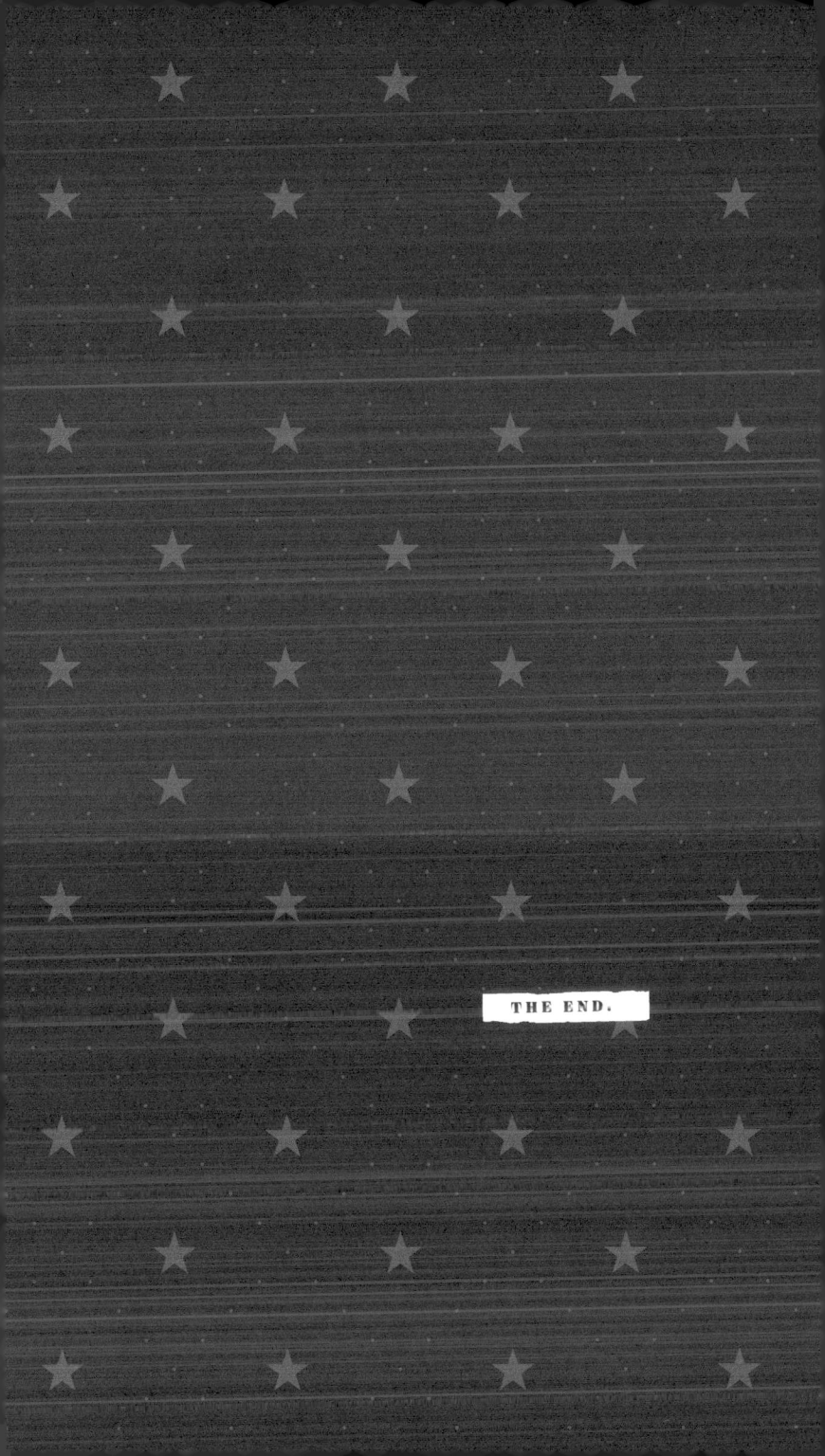

ACKNOWLEDGEMENTS

I MET JIM DICKINSON

in the mid-1990s, thanks to a timely introduction by publicist Jill Richmond who thought we'd hit it off. We did. Until Jim passed away in 2009, we talked on the phone every few weeks about music, Mississippi, art, philosophy, our families, you name it, and no trip to Memphis was complete without visiting Jim and Mary Lindsay at Zebra Ranch. Jim, on numerous occasions, spoke candidly about recording *Time Out of Mind* and Dylan's artistic process.

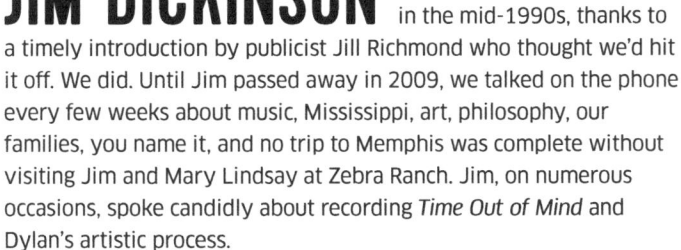

When I learned of the Bob Dylan Archive's (BDA) extensive *Time Out of Mind* holdings, I submitted a research proposal and jumped at the opportunity to go. BDA archivist/librarian Mark Davidson was an amiable and knowledgeable host, bringing out a steady stream of boxes, folders, and files and patiently answering questions. Mark also put me in touch with author Clinton Heylin, who'd previously visited the archive and helped me determine how much time I'd need to spend there. After my piece was written, David Beal at Special Rider coordinated the copyright clearances attentively and expeditiously. It was a pleasure dealing with these folks.

I'm aware that portions of the book may not jibe with others' opinions or even what some of the players experienced. My findings draw upon a multi-sourced mix of exclusive BDA material (from Dylan's handwritten notes to studio banter), Jim's firsthand accounts and insights, and a variety of additional sources.

I needed a designer and illustrator to interpret the text, and Amanda White-Iseli and Warren Linn came instantly to mind. Immensely talented, Amanda and Warren artfully convey meaning and mystery with appropriate levels of amplification and implication. Their work transcends the assignment's tight parameters and takes the entire project to another level. I can't thank them enough for generously sharing their time, talents, and opinions to forge such a rewarding collaboration.

I'd also like to thank Lydia Woolever, Max Weiss, and Jon Timian at *Baltimore* magazine, the Maryland State Arts Council for their support, Curt Iseli and Rupert Wondolowski for feedback on early drafts, and Wayne and Katy for their hospitality in Oklahoma. Mike Nakkula planted the idea of doing research at BDA during a memorable caffeine-fuelled conversation, and Mike Poletynski, my high school English teacher, planted the notion that I should care about Dylan. Mr. Poletynski drove a Volvo station wagon with "Dylan" plates and had the words "Give a Damn" mounted above the chalkboard in his classroom. It made an impression.

I've long admired the Dickinson family. Mary Lindsay championed Jim's work at every turn and called him "husband," because, well, anybody could call him "Jim." Luther and Cody earned their father's respect and admiration, as good people and as proponents of the Hill Country/Memphis music he loved. Luther and Cody's North Mississippi Allstars deserve your support *and* a Grammy Award. And anyone who hasn't read Jim's memoir, *I'm Just Dead, I'm Not Gone*, needs to remedy that.

Finally, I want to thank Anne, Posie, and Levi for everything, literally everything. You all make every day a whirly gig.

> **MR. POLETYNSKI DROVE A VOLVO STATION WAGON WITH "DYLAN" PLATES AND HAD THE WORDS "GIVE A DAMN" MOUNTED ABOVE THE CHALKBOARD IN HIS CLASSROOM. IT MADE AN IMPRESSION.**

JIM DICKINSON SELECT DISCOGRAPHY

SOLO RECORDINGS

I'm Just Dead, I'm Not Gone (live), Memphis Int'l, 2012
Dinosaurs Run in Circles, Memphis Int'l, 2009
Killers from Space, Memphis Int'l, 2007
Fishing with Charlie and Other Selected Readings, Birdman, 2006
Jungle Jim and the Voodoo Tiger, Memphis Int'l, 2006
Free Beer Tomorrow, Artemis, 2002
A Thousand Footprints in the Sand (live), Last Call, 1997
Delta Experimental Project Vol. II: Spring Poems, New Rose, 1990
Dixie Fried, Atlantic, 1972

PRODUCTION

North Mississippi Allstars, *Hernando*, Songs of the South, 2008
Boister, *Pieces of Milk*, Wing and a Prayer, 2002
T-Model Ford, *Bad Man*, Fat Possum, 2002
Giant Sand, *Chore of Enchantment*, Thrill Jockey, 2000
Mudhoney, *Tomorrow Hit Today*, Reprise, 1998
Screamin' Jay Hawkins, *At Last*, Last Call, 1998
Texas Tornados, *4 Aces*, Reprise, 1996
G. Love & Special Sauce, *Coast to Coast Motel*, Epic, 1995
Toots Hibbert, *Toots in Memphis*, Mango, 1988
The Replacements, *Pleased to Meet Me*, Sire, 1987
Big Star, *Third/Sister Lovers*, PVC, 1978
Ry Cooder, *Into the Purple Valley*, Warner Brothers, 1971

SESSION WORK

Jon Spencer Blues Explosion, *Acme*, Matador, 1998
Bob Dylan, *Time Out of Mind*, Columbia, 1997
Johnny Cash, "In Your Mind" (*Dead Man Walking* soundtrack), Columbia, 1996
Primal Scream, *Give Out but Don't Give Up*, Sire, 1994
Ry Cooder, *Paris, Texas* soundtrack, Warner Brothers, 1985
Maria Muldaur, *Maria Muldaur*, Reprise, 1973
Arlo Guthrie, *Hobo's Lullaby*, Reprise, 1972
Ronnie Hawkins, *The Hawk*, Cotillion, 1971
Flamin' Groovies, *Teenage Head*, Kama Sutra, 1971
The Rolling Stones, *Sticky Fingers*, Rolling Stones Records, 1971
Aretha Franklin, *Spirit in the Dark*, Atlantic, 1970
Carmen McRae, *Just a Little Lovin'*, Atlantic, 1970
Albert Collins, *Trash Talkin'*, Liberty, 1969

BDA MATERIAL REVIEWED BY AUTHOR

Bob Dylan Archive, Helmerich Center for American Research at Gilcrease Museum, Tulsa, Oklahoma, January 20-25, 2020.

SUBSERIES I (25): 1997

Box 101, Folder 07: "Mississippi" manuscript lyrics from the period of *Time Out of Mind*, circa 1997.

Box 101, Folder 08: "Highlands" manuscript lyrics from *Time Out of Mind*, circa 1997.

Box 101, Folder 09: "All I Ever Loved Is You" manuscript lyrics from *Time Out of Mind*, circa 1997.

Box 101, Folder 10: "Million Miles" manuscript lyrics from *Time Out of Mind*, circa 1997.

Box 101, Folder 11: "Dreamin' of You" lyrics from *Time Out of Mind*, circa 1997.

Box 102, Folder 01: "Cold Irons Bound" manuscript and typescript lyrics from *Time Out of Mind*, circa 1997.

Box 102, Folder 02: "Dirt Road Blues" manuscript lyrics from *Time Out of Mind*, circa 1997.

Box 102, Folder 03: "Things Have Changed" lyric fragment from *Time Out of Mind*, circa 1997.

Box 102, Folder 04: Unknown manuscript lyrics ("Until I Saw You. . .") from *Time Out of Mind*, circa 1997.

Box 102, Folder 05: "'Til I Fell in Love with You" manuscript lyrics from *Time Out of Mind*, circa 1997.

Box 102, Folder 06: "Love Sick" manuscript lyrics from *Time Out of Mind*, circa 1997.

Box 102, Folder 07: "Not Dark Yet" manuscript lyrics from *Time Out of Mind*, circa 1997.

Box 102, Folder 08: "Can't Wait" manuscript lyrics from *Time Out of Mind*, circa 1997.

Box 102, Folder 09: "Red River Shore" manuscript lyrics from *Time Out of Mind*, circa 1997.

Box 102, Folder 10: "Marching to the City" typescript lyrics from *Time Out of Mind*, circa 1997.

Box 102, Folder 11: Manuscript cover song lyrics ("I'm Free at Last," by Ernest Tubb) from the period of *Time Out of Mind*, circa 1997.

Box 102, Folder 12: Notes and unfinished lyrics from *Time Out of Mind*, circa 1997.

SUBSERIES III (4): 1990s

Box 98, Folder 03: Notes, writings, and unfinished lyrics, circa 1995–99.

SERIES X: CORRESPONDENCE

Box 39, Folder 10: Letter from Don Ienner (May 14, 1997)

RECORDING SESSIONS AND MASTER TAPES

Time Out of Mind. Sessions produced by Daniel Lanois and Jack Frost. January 1997, Criteria Studios, Miami, Florida; September-October 1996, The Teatro, Oxnard, CA.

*All items courtesy of The Bob Dylan Archive Collections, Tulsa, Oklahoma.

ADDITIONAL SOURCES

"Album of the Year: Time Out of Mind," *YouTube*,
Uploaded by Rusty Chalfont, May 8, 2018.

Bentley, Bill. *Fishing with Charlie and Other Selected Readings*
liner notes, Birdman Recording Group, 2006.

Dickinson, Jim (June 18, 1997 & September 30, 1997)
Interviews with the author.

Dickinson, Jim. *Free Beer Tomorrow* liner notes,
Artemis Records, 2002.

Dickinson, Jim, *I'm Just Dead, I'm Not Gone*. University Press
of Mississippi, 2017.

Dylan, Bob. *Chronicles: Volume One*. New York:
Simon & Schuster, 2004.

Epstein, Daniel Mark. *The Ballad of Bob Dylan*.
New York: HarperCollins, 2011.

Floyd, John. *Sun Records: An Oral History*.
New York: Avon, 1998.

Gates, David. "Dylan Lives," *Newsweek*, October 6, 1997.

Greene, Andy. "Inside Bob Dylan's Historic New Tulsa Archive,"
Rolling Stone, March 3, 2016.

Heylin, Clinton. *Still on the Road: The Songs of
Bob Dylan Vol. 2: 1974-2008*. London: Constable, 2010.

Howard, Mark. *Listen Up! Recording Music with Bob Dylan,
Neil Young, U2...* Toronto: ECW Press, 2019.

Levy, Joe. "Inside Bob Dylan's *Time Out of Mind* Sessions,"
Rolling Stone, September 30, 2017.

Lewis, John. "Jim Dickinson: L'homme de Memphis,"
Vibrations (April 2003).

Lewis, John. "Jim Dickinson," *Oxford American*
(Southern Music Issue, 1997).

Lewis, John. "Grey On Grey: Bob Dylan's New Album
Explores Mortality," Baltimore *City Paper* (October 1997).

Lewis, John. "Another Side of Bob Dylan," *VH1 Online* (Issue 11, 1997).

Mosley, Walter. *RL's Dream*. New York: W.W. Norton and Company, 1995.

Richards, Keith. *Life*. New York: Little, Brown and Company, 2010.

Tosches, Nick. *Country: The Twisted Roots of Rock n' Roll*.
New York: Da Capo Press, paperback edition, 1996.

**GRATEFUL ACKNOWLEDGEMENT
FOR THE FOLLOWING PERMISSIONS**

Unpublished *Time Out of Mind* archival material, Copyright © 2020 by Special Rider Music. All rights reserved. International copyright secured. Used with permission.

"Can't Wait" lyric, Copyright © 1997 by Special Rider Music. All rights reserved. International copyright secured. Reprinted by permission.

"Highlands" lyric, Copyright © 1997 by Special Rider Music. All rights reserved. International copyright secured. Reprinted by permission.

"Love Sick" lyric, Copyright © 1997 by Special Rider Music. All rights reserved. International copyright secured. Reprinted by permission.

"Mississippi" lyric, Copyright © 1996 by Special Rider Music. All rights reserved. International copyright secured. Reprinted by permission.

"Not Dark Yet" lyric, Copyright © 1997 by Special Rider Music. All rights reserved. International copyright secured. Reprinted by permission.

"Standing in the Doorway" lyric, Copyright © 1997 by Special Rider Music. All rights reserved. International copyright secured. Reprinted by permission.

"Tryin' to Get to Heaven" lyric, Copyright © 1997 by Special Rider Music. All rights reserved. International copyright secured. Reprinted by permission.

ABOUT THE CONTRIBUTORS

JOHN LEWIS is a writer and editor living in Cambridge, Maryland. He has profiled a wide range of cultural figures, from Ani DiFranco and Ira Glass to Lucille Clifton and the Wu-Tang Clan. His work has appeared in *Oxford American*, *Rolling Stone*, *Baltimore* magazine, and various other publications. Lewis received a Literary Arts award from the Maryland State Arts Council in 2022.

WARREN LINN began drawing at age 4 and hasn't stopped. A Chicago native, he has exhibited work at The Hyde Park Art Center and The Art Institute of Chicago and illustrated for *The New York Times*, *Rolling Stone*, *The New Yorker*, Sony Music, and many other outlets. He taught for 20 years at the Maryland Institute College of Art in Baltimore, where he has lived since 2002. Linn welcomes "the surprise of unintended discoveries" in his work.

AMANDA WHITE-ISELI's passion for graphic design is rivaled only by her love of music. After attending the Maryland Institute College of Art, she worked as an art director in Baltimore and Austin, Texas. Since returning to her home state and joining *Baltimore* magazine, her work, as creative director, has been recognized by the City Regional Magazine Association, the Maryland Society of Professional Journalists, and *Print* and *Folio* magazines.

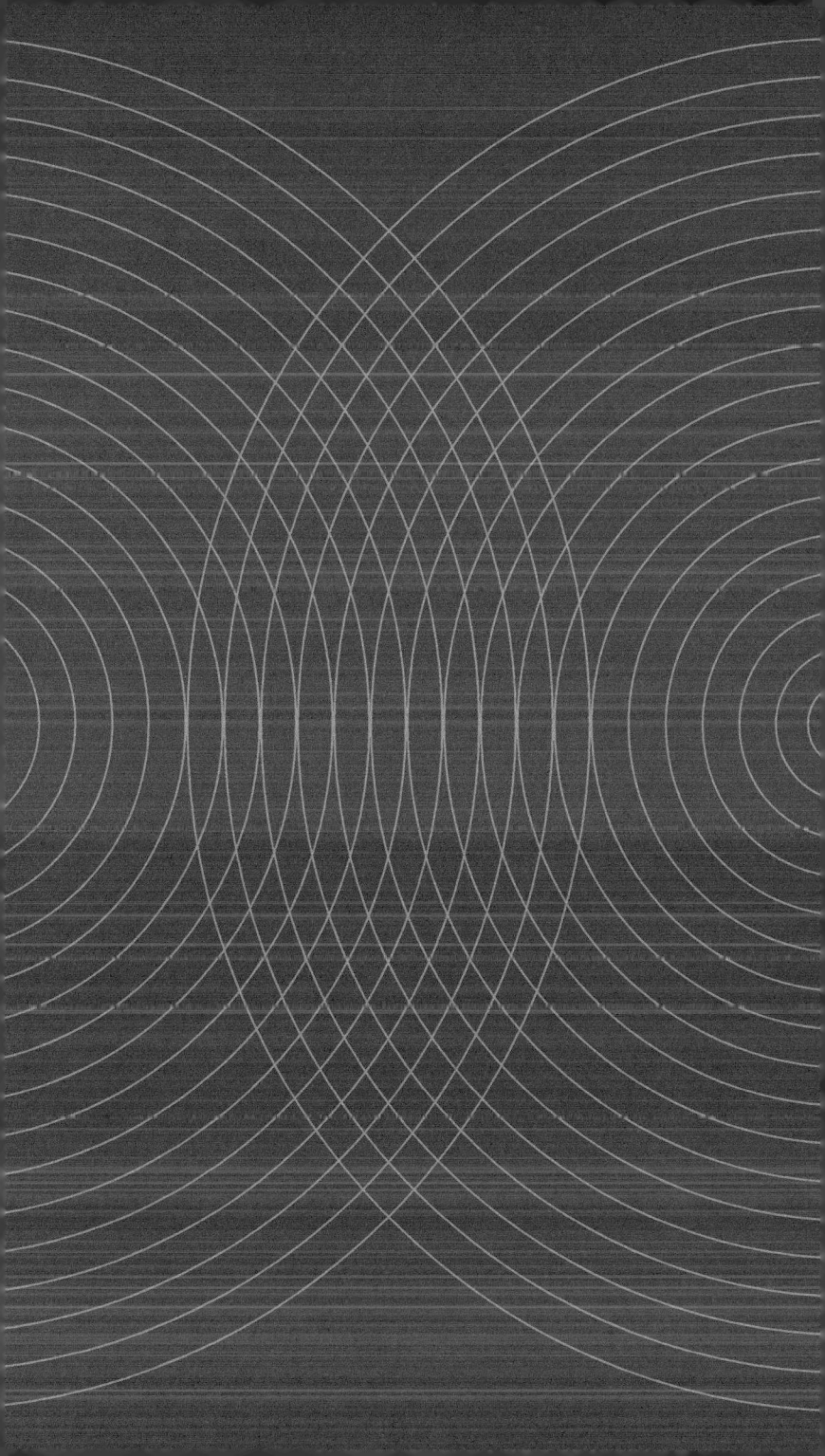

ILLUSTRATIONS BY WARREN LINN:
Cover and pages 5, 6, 19, 23, 31, 34, 37, 41, 43, 46, 50-51, 55, 65, 72-73, 77, 81 and 95.

W Linn